FADING HEARTS ON THE RIVER

FADING HEARTS ON THE RIVER

A LIFE IN HIGH-STAKES POKER

OR

HOW MY *SON* CHEATS
DEATH, WINS MILLIONS, & MARRIES
HIS COLLEGE *SWEETHEART*

BROOKS HAXTON

COUNTERPOINT
BERKELEY

Library of Congress Cataloging-in-Publication Data

Haxton, Bruce.
 Fading hearts on the river: a life in high-stakes poker / Bruce Haxton.
pages cm
 ISBN 978-1-61902-325-3 (hardback)
1. Poker. I. Title.

 GV1251.H28 2014
 795.412--dc23
 2013044915

ISBN 978-1-61902-325-3

Cover design by Matt Dorfman
Interior Design by Megan Jones Design

COUNTERPOINT
1919 Fifth Street
Berkeley, CA 94710
www.counterpointpress.com

Printed in the United States of America
Distributed by Publishers Group West

10 9 8 7 6 5 4 3 2 1

For my family, heart-winners each and all

Lucky and unlucky mean the same thing,
like flammable and inflammable.

—WILLIAM MATTHEWS

To *fade hearts on the river*, in Texas hold 'em,
is to avoid a heart on the final card,
so that the other player does not complete a flush in hearts
to win the hand.

CONTENTS

PARADISE ISLAND

where

ISAAC & ZOE

at the prospect of BIG CASH

CONTEND

with RISK and PLEASURE

in the *GAME*

UNDER THE FLOODLIGHTS on the veranda of the Atlantis Casino the chip leader leaned over the table, his face hidden behind dark glasses and shoulder-length brown hair. By the time I watched him on the video, I knew what was about to happen, because he was my son, Isaac, and this had been the start of his career in tournament play. But to see him in action, counting out chips and sliding a raise of more than $40,000 into the pot, felt unreal.

He still looked to me like one of the boys in a high-school grunge band. But the bloggers were calling him the Lizard King. At his age I would have killed to be taken for Jim Morrison, but I looked nothing like him. If you brush the hair back from his face and take off the dark glasses, Isaac looks like me: sensitive with his guard up, brainy and ironic.

His opponent, Ryan Daut, looked clean-cut, sad and pensive, almost monastic, sitting still with his head tilted to one side, hands folded, while he studied Isaac's body language. The raise was a problem in his mind. Ryan had come here on his break from the Ph.D. program in mathematics at Penn State. Isaac was taking time off after three years in computer science at Brown. The odds against either player making it this far into the tournament had been about five hundred to one.

Like them, I had planned for a time to teach college math, but I too took a chance instead. I spent hours every day writing poetry. I could see the odds: a tiny percentage of those who try to write memorable poems. Meanwhile, I wanted to support myself as a teacher of writing, and this was a long shot too. Playing against the odds in poetry has developed ways of thinking different from what poker requires of my son. Still, I want to understand him.

On the floodlit veranda the odds seemed to be turning in Isaac's favor, though the wind kept driving storm clouds over the lagoon and riffling the edges of hundred-dollar bills in bundles on the felt. A few summers earlier, both Ryan and Isaac had worked temporary jobs and spent their weekends with the other gaming geeks from their respective high schools, calculating strategy in StarCraft and Magic: The Gathering. Isaac and one of his closest friends were competitive against the best Magic players in the country.

When Ryan and his StarCraft friends took measurements one night, he once told an online interviewer, he took the honors, and that was why in his favorite poker forum, people knew him as BigBalls. In Isaac's favorite poker forum, people knew him as Ike, but his usual screen name at the tables was F33DMYB0NG, the logic behind which was to sound like such a brainless stoner that people would underestimate the intelligence of his play and make mistakes, which helped him, paradoxically, to feed his bong. More importantly, to my way of thinking, his opponents' errors had been paying his tuition.

Dozens of math nerds all over the world had taken silly screen names and started winning more per hour than most doctors and lawyers make. For each of these regular winners online, at any given time, by Ryan's estimate there were four losers. The losers burned out fast, but newcomers were plentiful.

In tournament play, as I was saying, the odds were worse. Among the 935 players who entered this tournament, including some of the most skillful in the world, 6 out of 7 lost the entry fee, leaving the prize pool for the others at more than $7 million. First place alone was $1,535,255, far more than I had earned in my whole life as a teacher and a writer. But for Ryan and Isaac the play of numbers and the flow of the game had more reality than what the numbers were supposed to represent.

In the next six years of tournament play Ryan and Isaac would not meet again at the final table. They would see each other only a few times. After this tournament, Ryan would win less than he spent on entry fees. His worst-case scenario for this evening, however, was to win $861,000, more than a hundred times what he had paid to enter. Several weeks earlier, Isaac had paid $175 to play a satellite online. By finishing first in the satellite, he had won a seat here in the main event, together with a trip to the Bahamas, all expenses paid. Now the smallest return Isaac could expect on his $175 was 500,000 percent.

With both players guaranteed to win so much, it might have been healthier to consider the money and the odds at this point inconceivable. What rattled me, as usual, was trying to make sense of things. The sum they would be divvying up in the next few hands was not quite $2.4 million. But it was slightly more than $2.397 million, $44 more. In my home game no one has ever won as much as $44.

Had I been there on the veranda with Isaac's girlfriend Zoe, where my wife Francie and our thirteen-year-old twin daughters were, just off the plane, it would have been unbearable for me to follow what came next. I would have been a wreck all day. It was difficult enough to think about it at a distance.

Isaac and Zoe told me later that he felt exhilarated when he went to meet the other players for the final table. Before she left the room that morning, Zoe had chosen an outfit, dressed, taken one last look, and started over. Later, on camera, she looked beautiful. But she was as anxious as I would have been. Every time she stood up at the rail, her head was swimming with huge sums of money risked on the fall of a single card. Her knees lost strength. They trembled. They were giving out. She understood the game, but she was too worked up to follow what was happening. Francie and our daughters Miriam and Lillie could follow less. Isaac's friends kept having to tell them what was going on.

From where I stood then, hundreds of miles away, it was impossible to watch at all. By the time the video was broadcast on the Travel Channel six months later, I knew what would happen, but even when I watch it now the match is a gut-wrencher toward the end.

And what happened after the match, none of us saw coming, not even Isaac, who would have told you then that he was keeping his eye on the ball.

❊

AT THE OPENING of an essay called "A Gambler for Life," David Mamet as a young man is visiting his father's downtown law office in Chicago when he realizes that his regular poker game, in a junk shop on the North Side (near where Zoe grew up), is about to start. He says he has to go.

His father wants to know, "For what?"

He says, "Gambling."

And his father asks him, "You still using the cards?"

Mamet's writing since then has become famous, in good part for the way he explores his father's question, which he takes to mean, "Can you not see that the game goes on around you all the time?"

Mamet, in any case, continued for some years to use the cards.

❊

AFTER THE ANNOUNCEMENT that the plane was landing, Zoe looked down into the clear blue water and thought how lucky it was that Isaac could bring her here to a tropical island, just by winning a poker game online. The two of them would have fun whether the tournament went well or not.

At the beginning of play on Friday, Day 1A of the 2007 PokerStars Caribbean Adventure, the tournament director issued the ceremonial command to the dealers at their tables, "Shuffle up and deal!" The tournament bloggers, whom I was following from hundreds of miles away, responded in the blogosphere with their own ceremonial message, "Cards are in the air."

The way to win big in a tournament is to get lucky, and Isaac got inordinately lucky. He doubled his chip stack, doubled that, and then won half that much again. This took nine hours. Tournament chips, in this early phase of play, technically were worth nothing. But they did represent potential, and at the end of his first day, Isaac, as a rookie, held the second-most potential in the room.

With Zoe he downplayed how well Day 1A had gone, which was not difficult, since she was used to hearing that Isaac had done well at the poker table. She told me later that the fun the two of them could have together on this trip still interested her more than Isaac's game. While I was writing this, I talked to her and Isaac many times for hours at a time about the details of their lives. At family get-togethers, I would interview them endlessly from long lists of questions, and they were more forthcoming than a nosy writer, or father, much less in-law, could reasonably ask.

The next afternoon, during the first day for the other half of the field, Day 1B, Isaac and Zoe went wading at the beach. He had spent nine hours the day before watching people watch each other work to control their faces, vocal tones, postures, and movements. Now, after two years together, he was watching Zoe, and he saw her in a different light. The modeling of her features looked the same. She was as beautiful as ever. She caught him watching her, and he saw the fullness of her lower lip cinched by the upper into an ironic smile, slightly deeper in the left corner of her mouth. There was something new in the lucidity of her green eyes, accented by the pale blue of the Caribbean. But the main thing he was noticing was the way she moved. She had been a dancer from the age of four. He was thinking that he wished he could move with half her poise. Poise did not matter when you played online, but at the tables, poise was everything.

After a little wading, with her long, caramel-brown hair blowing in her eyes, Zoe said it was too windy at the beach. It would be more relaxing in a big chair by the pool with an umbrella drink. She was reading *Love in the Time of Cholera*. Isaac was holding his book open, while he thought through the trickier hands he had played the day before. After a while, he interrupted Zoe.

In the book on her lap the passionate young lovers had separated, so that the heroine could make a more suitable marriage, and her husband, a man as rational and systematic as her lover had been passionate, was devoting himself to his work as a doctor.

Isaac asked about a certain hand, if Zoe thought that he might have gotten more chips with a bigger raise on the turn, or whether it would have been better to wait and bet more on the river, to give the other guy more-tempting odds. He told her every card that fell, and every bet and gesture.

When he finished, she said no. He did well to bet for value. He probably would have gotten less with a bigger bet.

He was wondering precisely how to calculate the differential.

In another spot, he thought, maybe he should have folded sooner. Or it might have made more sense to bluff. In either case, he wanted to be more precise about the probabilities, to play the best percentage every time. She thought he was doing well. It was a good call, she said. She was glad, at least, that he included her in his preoccupation.

It made sense that he would. Zoe knew him well, she had a head for numbers, and the math of poker interested her, at least theoretically. In college, after theater, math was her main concentration. At the moment, however, they were supposed to be relaxing on a tropical island. It was Isaac's day off from the tournament. He was not supposed to be playing the game steadily in his head. He was beginning to think, he said, that he might want to go inside, just to see how they were doing with Day 1B.

Zoe understood that he was still uneasy with the differences between the game online, which he had played for three years daily, and the live game, which he had played much less. She did not consider that the odds against finishing his first day with one of the top two stacks, if the results were truly random, would have been two hundred to one. Isaac was not superstitious, but he would have talked about his chances of staying near the lead no more than a pitcher in the dugout after the fifth inning would discuss the chances of another inning toward his perfect game. Any strict analysis of probabilities concludes that the idea of a streak, in sports or gambling, is an illusion. But competitors, superstitious or not, even serious students of mathematics, all know in their bones that it is very foolish to do anything that might *jinx* a streak.

That night, they ate at the Italian restaurant in the resort. It cost, Isaac noted, three times as much as any place they ate in Providence. But he was glad for them to be there, sharing food this good and having fun.

Before the cards were in the air on Day 2, with Zoe at breakfast telling him her plans, Isaac had withdrawn. Head bowed over a plate of eggs he left untouched, face hidden behind his hair, sullen and unresponsive, he looked up slowly into the distance, stood, and left her in the restaurant alone. This was first time she had seen what she now calls Isaac's tournament mode, and it made her fume. It took a while to walk it off. She was exploring the resort. When she felt better, she relaxed and swam again in the pool. She did some reading.

When she tried visiting the casino, this was the first time she heard the sound of so many players shuffling their chips at once. An individual shuffle is a rapid succession of tiny clicks. A tournament multiplies this sound into the roar of human cicadas in one of those years when millions hatch at once.

She looked around the edges of the room away from the tournament floor, and everywhere she looked were players' girlfriends. Some of them stood looking on, their faces blank. Their boyfriends sat among the hundreds of players at dozens of table. From here it was impossible to follow what the players were doing. Some of the girlfriends were knitting. A few of them were together talking. Zoe went back to the pool and read. Six hours later, still alone, she watched the full moon rise into the palm trees.

While Isaac was immersed in the details of his opponents' behavior at the table, Zoe was living the imaginary lives of lovers in the mind of Gabriel Garcia Marquez. Fermina's husband, the doctor, betrayed her

once with another woman, while she betrayed him steadily with her
unconsummated love for the passionate Florentino, who dreamed of
Fermina for his whole life, despite many affairs.

After nine hours of play on Day 2, Isaac was in fourteenth place
among the 121 players remaining. When he got back to the hotel room,
again he downplayed his success, which was easy to do, because fourteenth place sounded far less favorable than fifth, where he had started
the day, 3 more players having finished ahead of him on Day 1B.

In fact, fourteenth place was extraordinarily good. Three-fourths
of the surviving players had been eliminated on Day 2, while Isaac
had been tripling his stack. Only 7 of the top 20 from the beginning
of Day 2 had survived the day, and Isaac was still in a position where
one hand might place him in the lead. But what he emphasized to Zoe
was not the considerable chance of going deep enough to win big. He
told her he was in the money. If he went all in and busted in the very
next hand, he would win almost $12,000. This was the worst that he
could do, not bad.

It hardly registered to her that he was doing well. She needed to tell
him how he had hurt her feelings. That morning his mind had been so
disconnected from the moment with her and so set on the game about
to begin, he could not remember having done what she described. But
he understood what she was saying. He was responsible for having
hurt her feelings, and he saw exactly how she felt. He was sorry.

Meanwhile, he was fascinated by her way of expressing herself.
He had been watching people today for nine hours, analyzing them,
and now he could not seem to stop. Zoe had the clear inflections of
an actor who has grown into the contours of her voice. She had studied drama for years, and Isaac was thinking about this. Her beauty

distracted him, of course. He could have used that kind of beauty at the table, if he had it. What he could really use at the table was her poise and skill, not, in his case, for the sake of transparency, not for the clarity of what she was expressing now, but more nearly for the opposite. He needed to become opaque.

But that was not what mattered now. Now he was apologizing. It was the pressure of the tournament, he said. It took him somewhere else, that's all. He wanted to make it up to her, to forget poker. They should go out for the most extravagant meal that they had ever shared, the tasting menu at Nobu.

To reckon what they could afford, Isaac told me, instead of forgetting poker, he was figuring his equity in the tournament so far. *Equity* is the term a poker player uses for his probabilistic share of the money at stake. If he has a 50 percent probability of winning a hand, he calls this a 50 percent equity in the total pot for that hand. An effective player keeps putting money into the pot only so long as his equity remains greater than the sum of what he bets. This principle is called *pot odds*. The incompleteness of the information available and the fact that equity keeps changing while the hand unfolds can make the calculation ticklish.

To figure equity in a tournament is trickier than figuring for one hand, and Isaac was a little foggy on the quantification. He came up, improvising in his head, with a wildly optimistic figure as his equity after day two. It so happened that he would win ten times that figure, but less than a tenth of it, luckily, would have covered the tasting menu for two at Nobu every evening of their stay.

When I was interviewing Isaac and Zoe one last time, six years after the evening in question, I wanted to hear everything they could remember. Isaac said that he had told me all he knew, but Zoe would do better.

She said it would help for readers to understand her confidence when she told Isaac he had hurt her feelings. She knew he would listen. They told each other how they felt, and they both listened. This made their connection strong. Isaac was listening while she told me this. When she stopped, he nodded.

I asked him if what she was saying reminded him of anything more, and he looked down, with a vague shake of the head. "I'm not very good with remembering personal interactions."

Zoe and I both started laughing.

He was looking sheepish. "I remember poker hands," he said. "I remember all the Magic cards ever printed." He was being funny now, but there was something underneath.

"Yeah," I said. "You remember the whole rule book in Magic verbatim. What is it, two hundred pages?"

"I remember it"—he gave Zoe an ironic smile—"in all its iterations." Isaac underplays his social skills. But at the moment, by making fun of himself, he was reaffirming his apologies to her, because he knows his preoccupations can be difficult.

She and I both understood this, and we kept laughing. He was laughing too.

After shaking his head, he tried an upbeat tone. "I'm very good with the names of fish."

This made Zoe gasp. "Yes, he *is* good with fish, all the menus, all the different languages . . ."

At Nobu, they were just embarking on their lifelong seafood explorations, and from the description of the dishes on the menu, they had their doubts. For one thing, they saw that their first course would be raw oysters on the half shell with Nobu sauces. They had tried raw oysters only once before, and they were not quite sure, but they both felt adventurous. The chef, Nobu Matsuhisa, after living in Peru, had dreamed up these assorted salsas of chopped onions, one of them with tomato, orange, and chili paste, another with parsley, vinegar, chili oil, and chili garlic sauce. A third used jalapeños finely chopped rather than chili paste, this one with lemon and olive oil. A cool, raw oyster topped with any of these salsas was, as Isaac and Zoe soon agreed, the stuff of heaven. At Nobu on Paradise Island everything was heaven. It was the best meal they had ever shared, and it was clear, from how they joked about the oysters as an aphrodisiac, that they had put their misunderstanding over breakfast far behind them.

※

DESPITE MY PARENTS' recent divorce, when Francie and I were in our thirties, after ten years together, we felt that it was high time we had children. Francie could take a year's leave from medical school to be with the baby. After that, it would be painful for her to spend long hours away while she finished her training, but she could manage, and I could do the lion's share of the parenting.

The spring Isaac was two, I taught half-time at Sarah Lawrence College. When I finished for the day and walked out under an ancient wisteria arbor onto the South Lawn where he was playing with his babysitter and her friends, he was having fun, and I was glad to have gotten a break from child care. But the easy pleasure in our first connecting glance gratified me to a depth I cannot describe. It was lucky. I would have spent less time with him under different circumstances and never would have known what I was missing.

Five years after the tournament in the Bahamas, Isaac was living with Zoe in a high-rise on Dean Martin Boulevard overlooking the Strip. His sisters were living in Syracuse in the house where he had grown up, finishing their senior year in the high school he had attended. Before long Francie and I would be missing them all every day and now, in my perpetual effort to make sense of things, I began to write this story. At my desk I could be absorbed again in Isaac's company, in the strangeness of what he did and how he came to do it. When I read passages aloud to Lillie, Miriam, and Francie, we felt Isaac coming back to us out of the distance.

❀

THE FATHER OF my best friend from early childhood was a professional poker player, an alcoholic, and a deadbeat. I could not believe that my friend in her twenties made her living at the bridge table. Her appetite for gaming, like my son's, must have been inherited, but I find poker an improbable profession, even so.

Ethics, for me, is not the point. My job is to offer a liberal arts education in exchange for tuition most people cannot afford. I have chosen to indulge myself in work I happen to find pleasing. To take a superior attitude toward the ethics of poker players, in my case, and in the case of almost everyone I know, would be hypocritical.

When acquaintances ask after Isaac, some of them express amazement that the gifted child whose bar mitzvah party they attended would be spending years of his life at the poker table. The strangeness of what happens can provoke a gratifying mix of empathy and wonder. But sometimes the empathy in questions about Isaac goes astray. Some of my acquaintances seem disappointed, as if on my behalf. They cannot believe that my son has squandered his gifts. They judge him as I judge my old friend's deadbeat dad. But playing poker has not made Isaac a deadbeat, or a thief, or a cheat.

Risking money at the poker table is similar in its ethics to taking part in an economy sustained by the investment industry. Investors profit from risks based on more or less dubious representations of value. People who know Wall Street compare investing to poker. The rest of us pay taxes in return for benefits derived from this risk-driven economy. To pay taxes oneself and to disapprove of others playing poker is absurd. Money is the game, and everybody plays. We hope the game is honest, but we know better.

My father sold men's clothing at Nelms and Blum in Greenville, Mississippi. The ethics of working to distribute madras shirts and Bass Weejuns in the poorest state in the Union did not weigh heavily on anyone's conscience in my family. For our purposes, to do good work was to sell more shoes and shirts. My brothers and I helped. Retailing in our family was an honest living, but it was not, for any of us, a very interesting game. My father made the best of it by sustaining a steady fascination with the people around him. In the sixties, in a small town in the South, my father was such an oddball that it surprised nobody when he grew a beard in middle age. He made his eccentricities a play-ful part of salesmanship. As an older man he let his hair hang to his shoulders. Still, he went to work six days a week in a coat and tie.

Once his sons were grown and he had helped to get us started in the world, he retired early, to live on Social Security and to dedicate himself to other games, including the arts. He was an amateur composer, musical performer, writer, sculptor, and a director of plays and musicals. Meanwhile, he earned a little extra after retirement by composing some of the most difficult and inventively designed crosswords published by *The New York Times*. Toward the end of his life, his income placed him below the poverty line. His house was in poor repair, but he lived well.

Our family liked to play all kinds of games. At twelve, I saved money from mowing lawns to buy a regulation-size pool table, which my parents let me keep in the playroom, a converted garage. I loved to play eight ball, rotation, cutthroat, and, especially, straight pool. My fascination with the game has nothing to do with gambling. The geometry of the table, the physics of the spins, banks, and collisions, everything about it pleases me.

My older brother, Richard, used to organize big poker games. Unbeknownst to their parents, his friends played at our house for as much as they could scrape together, and Richard often won. I never did play cards with them, but the house rules were that the winner in a game of pool stayed at the table to play the next challenger, and I got to stay at the table most of the time. I thought I might become a serious player, but soon enough, I found that a hot shot with my skills is known by serious players as the local talent, which means fish.

A few years later, at the height of the Vietnam War, after he had enjoyed the extracurriculars for two years of college, Richard found himself playing a very different kind of game in the Georgia woods at night. By volunteering for the army just ahead of the draft and excelling in Officer Candidate School, he was hoping to improve his chances of avoiding combat. On the night in question he made his way along a path so dark that he could hardly see his feet. Enemy campfires shone far off through trees and undergrowth. If you have walked through deep woods in the dark, you know how it feels to be spooked by sounds of unknown creatures moving near you. Richard was hearing screams of men who had been captured. They were enduring simulated torture. His adrenalin was off the chart when one of the enemy team sprang onto the dark path just in front of him and started to tell him he was captured. Richard was too deeply locked into war-game mode, and his reflexes from training were too quick, to stop what followed. He swiveled the rifle in his grip, swiped the buttstock into the enemy's face, and broke the man's jaw. To see this happening was just a hint of the effects of having trained so thoroughly for such a game.

My brother Ayres may be the most competitive of us. A flat-track motorcycle racer for several years after he dropped out of college, he crashed many times, and he broke bones, as everyone in flat-track racing did. Friends of his were killed. Ayres gave it up in time, luckily, to raise his children. Still he likes to compete in political races, where he has been a winning candidate and a consultant. Now, as a lawyer, he competes against opposing counsel.

Gaming is a family trait. My mother's father played football at Ole Miss, and my father's father, who was an All-American quarterback on the same team a few years later, was state golf champion twice and made a hole in one in his seventies. My mother played cards and liked solving puzzles. Her sister was a Life Master in bridge and played skillfully past the age of eighty. A champion debater as a girl, my mother grew up to be an award-winning writer of fiction and nonfiction. For me, as for her, writing is inescapably competitive and more game-like than some of my fellow writers like to think. My wife's family has its roster of strong competitors as well, in all kinds of play, including sport, science, chess, law, and business. Her father was a lawyer and part owner of a racetrack. But even for a gamer like me from a family of gamers, poker looks peculiar as a way of life for my son.

※

BY SUNSET ON Day 3, Isaac had more than tripled his stack when he called an all-in bet and won with nothing but a pair. That pot sent him up from a decisive lead into the stratosphere.

The bloggers interviewed his friends. They reported how old he was, what he studied, where he went to school, how much he played online, and at what stakes.

He won two more huge hands, and when play stopped at nine o'clock, with sixteen players left, Isaac held 20 percent of the chips, twice as much as the player in second place.

After that, when he talked to Zoe, there was no downplaying how things went. Strangers had been stopping her in the hall to introduce themselves and ask if she was Isaac Haxton's girlfriend. It was time, she thought, and he agreed, for another meal at Nobu. As a friend who studied finance had told Isaac after a big win online, "This is great. You can buy a taco now whenever you want one." Isaac's equity in the tournament by this point had landed him in the region of unlimited tacos.

Friends of Isaac and Zoe's from college joined them. Jared Okun, who had washed out in this tournament, sat quietly with his girlfriend celebrating Isaac's luck. Jared had cashed the previous year in three World Series tournaments and would cash in four more the following year. Scott Seiver, who had cashed in tournaments before, was also busted, and he would win much less than what Isaac or Jared won that year, but his tournament winnings in the subsequent four years, at more than a million a year, would exceed Isaac's by a healthy margin. Without the crystal ball I use for predicting the past, all three analyzed the game, compared their own skills to those of the successful players, saw the amounts of money changing hands, and concluded, it made sense for them to play. This analysis was borne out for all three of them. Most of the players who thought that they had thought this through lost everything they put at stake.

Isaac and Zoe, after the oysters, shared various sushi plates. They were passionate converts. When I asked Zoe how she felt that evening, she told me that she was having as much fun watching Isaac as she was eating the sushi. When people visited the table to shake Isaac's hand and wish him luck, what she had loved about him for two years, his good-natured confidence, his calm intelligence, was so steady, he could not have been more pleasingly himself. Elated at the moment, but not shaken by excitement, she told me, he exuded, more than the impression of power, an actual scent, an essence that lifted off his skin and made her lean in closer for another breath.

※

THE RULES IN Texas hold 'em say that each player, dealt two cards face-down, makes the best possible five-card hand, using either, neither, or both of these two cards, unknown to the other players, and any, or all, of five common cards dealt face-up in the center of the table.

In the casino, where the dealer stays in the same chair and does not deal himself a hand, the button, which is a disk that marks the changing order of the deal and of the betting, rotates around the table hand by hand. The betting begins with two unequal blind bets, posted before the deal by the two players to the immediate left of the button. The rest of the betting follows the four stages of the deal: (1) after the two hole cards; (2) after the first group of three common cards, called the flop; (3) after the fourth common card, called the turn; and (4) after the final common card, called the river.

In my home game, a white chip is 25¢, a red chip 50¢, and a blue chip $1. Because the bets are limited, the most foolhardy player loses less than $20 in a long night's game.

A *tournament* chip, on the other hand, unlike the chips in cash games, cannot be redeemed. Players stay in the tournament until they lose their last chip, and prize money is awarded according to the player's finishing position, second, third, fourth, and so on. It is incorrect to assign an absolute value to a tournament chip. Only the place at the finish has absolute value. But, since Isaac and Ryan were playing heads-up for the difference between first and second place, a difference of $673,466, a single one of their nineteen million chips could be considered worth approximately three and a half cents.

I would never think to minimize the value of *their* chips as compared to those in *my* home game. Three and a half cents is much less than a quarter. This is true. But they were young men, and I have no wish to humiliate them.

The sizes of the pots they played were large by anybody's measure. For the betting I am about to describe, a bet of one million tournament chips is roughly comparable to a bet of $35,000. This is ten thousand

times the size of a respectable pot in my game, and more than I have
made in royalties on all my books of poetry in forty years of writing
every day.

I will give the value of the bets in monetary sums, misleading as
this is, because, for me, the money makes the story more excruciating, and I am, like all writers and all gamblers, deeply committed to
things excruciating.

❊

WHEN ISAAC'S HEAD would not come out, Francie, who was
laboring without anesthetic, told me that she wanted to deliver in the
squatting position. She had studied midwifery. She knew that gravity
helps, and she needed help. We spread a sheet on the linoleum of the
storage closet floor, the only room they had for us at St. Vincent's
Hospital, and I supported Francie's weight from behind by planting
my feet far apart, bending my knees, hooking my elbows under her
armpits, and leaning back. Isaac's weight and Francie's contractions
together tore him a way out into the world, and the midwife caught
him when he dropped.

Both my hands, and my arms from the elbows down, were numb
by then, but I was feeling lucky. Francie, whose risk of seizure had been
elevated by preeclampsia, suffered injuries no worse than those from
most healthy labors, and Isaac was amazing, handsome as Wallace
Shawn is handsome, in a way that mixes comedy, pathos, and wisdom.

On the slow drive from the hospital up the West Side of Manhattan
to our apartment, just north of the Bronx, my sense of dread, while I
steered to avoid potholes, was almost as deep as before and during

labor. It baffled me that they would let us, without experience as parents, take this sweet and vulnerable person out into the dangerous world only fourteen hours after he was born.

A few days later, Isaac's pediatrician sent him directly from an office appointment to the neonatal intensive care unit of the teaching hospital for the Albert Einstein Medical College in the Bronx. This was before cell phones. I was informed by messenger in the middle of teaching my first poetry workshop at Sarah Lawrence College. In tears, I sped directly to the hospital.

Although newborn jaundice as a rule is fleeting and innocuous, Isaac's skin was the sickly yellow of an old bruise, and the toxicity of his blood rose steadily toward the level where, the experts told us, permanent brain damage would set in. Every time one of the nurses reached into the transparent plastic box where they were keeping him and jabbed his heel for another blood test, he began to bawl, and Francie wept. She weeps now when I mention it.

When the bilirubin level rose to eighteen milligrams in one deciliter of blood, this was the standard indicator for a total exchange transfusion. They would remove all of Isaac's blood through an umbilical catheter and replace it with blood products from the hospital. But the blood products frightened us as much as the bilirubin. In 1985 the Bronx was one of the hotspots for the AIDS epidemic, then at its height. There was also a mysterious new form of hepatitis, another blood-borne disease which had been observed clinically, but not yet isolated, the disease now known as hepatitis C, a potentially fatal condition highly resistant to treatment and often intractable.

We were trying, as Isaac does now when he faces an important bet, to calculate with incomplete information the probability of various outcomes. We knew that any action, whether we did the math or not, would have to be predicated on our understanding of probabilities.

In the spring of 1985, three years after the first known case of a baby infected with HIV from transfused blood, the FDA had approved a blood test for HIV. Blood products in hospitals had been declared safe just a few weeks before Isaac needed them. But the virus for hepatitis C was still a mystery. It had as yet no name, no test existed, and none would exist for six years. Since the disease appeared to remain dormant, sometimes for a decade or much more, the likelihood of infection was anybody's guess.

Francie had been working for fifteen years as a nurse's aide, a nurse, a teacher of nursing, and now as a medical student. Incurable illnesses were not for her a vague reality on television. Her view of HIV and of the new strain of hepatitis involved, more than abstract dread, memories of men and women she had treated while they died.

How the recently declared level of safety for blood products might be measured in the long run, she told me, was not clear. The official declaration of safety represented risks measured by doctors concerned about large numbers of patients. But for an individual patient, for Isaac, who was sleeping not in his mother's arms but in this terrifying Isolette, this plastic box, the acceptable risk might differ from what is deemed acceptable on the larger scale. Isaac, as opposed to a general population of patients, would not generate a favorable proportion of differing outcomes. He had one chance. If he got unlucky his one time and died, the low probability of that outcome would make no difference for him. I could hardly speak. I felt unsteady on my feet and seasick.

The doctors in the ICU were insisting that we do the total exchange. They said our only other choice was to accept the crippling effects of the toxin in Isaac's brain. When I asked, they said they could not use my blood on such short notice, though I am a universal donor, because testing was mandatory. I asked if a waiver was possible, and they said not. My helplessness and ignorance felt something like a trance. These doctors, as far as I could tell, were intelligent, dedicated, and excellent at their job. But I trusted Francie's judgment more than I did theirs.

Francie was insisting, although no one mentioned this alternative, that we exchange half of Isaac's blood for an equal volume of saline to dilute the bilirubin. Blood is, after all, nine-tenths salt water. The partial exchange would remove half the toxin and lower the level of toxin that remained in proportion to the overall volume of blood. This would slow the metabolism of hemoglobin and give Isaac a chance to make more good blood for himself. If this failed, Francie told me, we could still consider a transfusion with blood products. The terrible likelihood, after all, was that the source of the problem, which no one understood, would keep causing it. No one knew how many transfusions would be necessary. Sometimes this scenario ends with infant death. Isaac, under the glare of the bili-lights, screamed and waved his arms. Nobody knew precisely what was happening in his brain.

Disagreement about the most effective stopgap, meanwhile, was intense, and the vehemence on both sides rang in everybody's voice. The doctors described the risks in grisly terms. Francie, while she listened to them, nodded steadily, as she often does when others speak, as if the physical act of nodding generated empathy and understanding on both sides. But she refused the permission necessary for the use of blood products, and I stood behind her, while the doctors shot wild looks my way, in hope that I might reason with her, or take charge. She understood their arguments as well as they did, and she disagreed.

When neither of us budged, they finally acceded to Francie's plan, and it worked.

In short, we played the cards as they were dealt. Francie happened to have the presence of mind and the expertise to play them with great skill, and we got lucky. No one knew what caused the problem, but as inexplicably as it arrived, it vanished.

When Lillie and Miriam were born, and Lillie developed the same condition, with precisely the same high level of bilirubin in her blood, the doctor suggested that Francie might be one of fewer than a dozen mothers in the world ever reported to have this syndrome of severe but fleeting hyperbilirubinemia in their newborn children. Because the danger level for elevated bilirubin had been revised by then slightly upward, none of the doctors at the hospital with Lillie thought that a transfusion was necessary. This, for her, was the luck of the draw.

I am not arguing that medical science is a game of chance. To think of the world primarily as a game is appalling. Einstein rejected the philosophical implications of the randomness in quantum mechanics, even though his own insight that light behaves as if it came in particles as well as waves, both at once, although these two representations appeared mutually exclusive, anticipated the development of quantum mechanics and, thus, its philosophical implications. Einstein said later that "the Old One," his name for the ultimate cosmic power, "does not throw dice." The logical crux of this statement for a scientist like Einstein, who did not believe in God, might have involved some gamesmanship. But Einstein's refusal to accept a way of thinking that devalues the idea of consequence and choice has always struck me as admirable. Probability, nevertheless, is one of the great mysteries of being.

In Isaac's case, mathematical ability, like fleeting hyperbilirubine-mia, must come from an improbable combination of genes. His mind-set under pressure, I believe, is inherited largely from his mother, who has never taken an interest in games.

For reasons Einstein would approve, Isaac does not throw dice. He uses the cards.

ON DAY 4 Zoe tried watching from the rail.

Within ten minutes, Isaac was dealt pocket aces, the best possible cards, which come, on average, once in every 221 hands. At a table with eight players, each of them can expect to see pocket aces about once every seven hours on average. Aces are most deadly when someone else has a premium hand to bet against them, which tends to happen less than half the time or, for each player, once every fourteen hours. This time, luckily for Isaac, someone else was holding an ace and a king, a combination that will beat 15 out of 16 random hands. Against AA, however, AK loses, after the rest of the cards are dealt, twelve in thirteen times. This was one of the twelve. Isaac won three hundred thousand chips, eliminating Joe Marcal, who got $45,915 for sixteenth place.

After a few more hands, the player in second place held pocket kings, a favorite against every hand but the one that Isaac happened to be holding, pocket aces, again. In a six-handed game, only one in every forty-four pairs of pocket kings will face pocket aces. This would be once every three hundred hours for a particular player or once, maybe, in ten tournaments. In that rare case, aces beat kings, after all the cards are dealt, four out of five times. Isaac won two million chips.

Isaac's heater was exactly what Zoe had been wanting to see, better than anyone could have predicted, but the rail made her too nervous to stay put. To follow the game from the rail, without knowing the contents of any of the hands, was almost as boring as it was nerve-wracking. She walked to steady her nerves, came back, walked, came back, and then, finally, she decided to follow the match online from the bed in their room, where she felt less rattled. By nightfall, Isaac had doubled his stack again to more than nine million chips.

✳

IN 1654, AFTER the lead horses on his carriage bolted, plunged through the railing of a bridge, and almost dragged the whole rig after them into a fatal crash, according to one story, Blaise Pascal repented his life until then as a serious gambler. But his calculations about gambling mattered more than he knew, first in the development of infinitesimal calculus and then, hundreds of years later, in genetics, post-Einsteinian physics, and computer science.

Pascal himself used his calculus of probability away from the gaming table not for science, but to make an argument for religious faith. He reasoned that we should "wager" in our mortal ignorance, by risking faith in the divine, because the potential reward is infinite and the liability not great. This is the most famous calculation of pot odds in the history of gambling. In Isaac's case, the money at the final table was not infinite, but it was enough, I thought, to justify my bringing Pascal's wager back to the green felt where it belonged.

I could not be there at the rail with Francie, Miriam, Lillie, and Zoe, because I was committed to give a lecture on the poems I had been translating. But I was at the rail in spirit when I introduced my lecture by praising the generosity of the gods of chance. The irrelevance of the introduction confused my audience. But I was prepared, agnostic though I am, to believe with Pascal that placing a public wager of faith on the side of the gods might help.

A little way into the actual lecture, I had to stop. I looked down nervously into the page on the lectern, and I excused myself for a minute. The audience, which included several famous writers and translators, looked baffled by my stumbling apology. They began to mumble while I made an exit, stage left. Soon, I was at the computer terminal in the next room, relieved to be checking the tournament results online.

※

POKER CAN BE a difficult way of life. If you are a reasonable person in a major poker tournament, you look at the cards and fold, hand after hand after hand. You may bluff once in a great while. Mainly, you wait. After being patient for hours, you get it in with pocket aces. This was what you hoped for. Now, though, even when your odds are four to one, as good as anyone could reasonably ask, you can expect to lose, one time in five.

When a blustering half-wit hits lucky for the third time running, you may feel frustration and resentment start to well. But to indulge your righteousness at this point is weak thinking. Your best move is to laugh like the hapless loser which you really are and to congratulate the winner, with good-humored envy, on his play. You want the half-wit to feel good about making plays against the odds. In the long run, if he does this, he will lose.

In a major tournament career, every reasonable player in the field expects to lose most of the time. For the most skillful, over the years, the sum of the winning results, a single one of which may be more than a hundred times the size of the buy-in, will exceed the sum of the buy-ins. To avoid frustration, meanwhile, to feel gratified by playing, win or lose, Isaac tries to play with skill. Recklessness, by definition, is weak thinking. But the appearance of recklessness may draw others into vulnerable patterns of play. Excessive caution also is weak thinking. But the appearance of caution affords opportunities for deception. The challenge is to choreograph a dance of appearances, with a dance of probabilities and a dance of actions.

The difficulty of accepting unpredictable results gets everybody down from time to time. But gamblers have no special standing in the realm of trouble. Writers and artists like to say how hard it is to live with their uncertainties. But food batch-makers, I have read, are the workers most at risk for suicide. Doctors, at the opposite end of the spectrum in education and in income, are not far behind. These statistics may be unreliable. Dentists, they say, have high rates of suicide and addiction. Dentists may need therapy, but therapists are just as bad. Truck drivers can tell you about truck drivers. Cops know how things go for cops, soldiers for soldiers. Anybody who chooses a career is playing the odds. As for saints, according to reliable reports, they tend to be sick puppies too. Look how often they choose martyrdom. But I hope they pray for us all.

※

BY MIDAFTERNOON, I was following the bloggers' commentary on the tournament from a desk in a dorm room saturated with sandalwood incense, burned not by me in honor of Ganesh or other gods of fortune, or of writing, but by someone else a few weeks earlier. The two undergraduates who shared this room were gone now between semesters. Their clothes, books, computers, speakers, sports equipment, musical instruments, and so forth, all redolent of sandalwood, were heaped chin-high in half the room, and I was staying now for ten days in the other half. During residencies for the master's program in creative writing, I have stayed in the dorms at Warren Wilson College in North Carolina on a regular basis for twenty years. No one could have predicted, when I was living in a dorm in 1968 and burning incense with my friends, that other friends of mine and I would be staying in other dorms forty years later, and that undergraduates in the twenty-first century would have decorated their rooms with posters of our long-dead idols, Janis Joplin, Jimi Hendrix, and Jim Morrison. The world is a confluence of improbabilities.

I sat with my laptop at one of the desks, reading the live blogs about the tournament as they were posted, one every five minutes or so. Isaac had three-fourths of the chips, and Ryan had the rest. I kept pressing Refresh, to read the latest post as soon as possible.

At the moment, while I leaned in to read on the computer that the final table was down to two players, Isaac and Ryan had stopped playing cards to observe a ceremony involving four Bahamian models in little black dresses.

Francie, Miriam, and Lillie were standing with Zoe at the rail. The day before, as soon as she was able to book three plane tickets to Nassau, Francie had withdrawn the girls from school in the middle of class. The director of the middle school followed the three of them into the parking lot declaiming in her best administrative tone that a trip to the Bahamas is *not* a family emergency. Francie, like any sane mother in these circumstances, had to disagree.

So there they were, to watch the Zion Zynergy Girls bring in the sheaves, packets of hundred-dollar bills on silver trays, soon heaped on the table within the players' reach. The first time the models sashayed past Isaac in high heels and tipped their bundles onto the tabletop, as luck would have it, the camera was not running. So they collected the money, took it back inside, rearranged it for display, and on cue they brought it out again.

When they were done, Isaac, laughing, picked up one of the stray bundles, which had fallen into his chips, and he tossed it backhand onto the heap. On video I have watched him do this several times. Everything about his body language says that he felt set to win.

When I asked him later how he felt to see the money within reach, he told me that he felt incredulous. He started wondering how much it was. He guessed, there must be forty bundles. Assuming that each bundle was $10,000, as they appeared to be, this whole heap would have added up to less than the difference between first and second place. If this were the actual $2.4 million at stake, he was thinking, the heap of hundred-dollar bills would have covered the table and weighed more than a hundred pounds.

But when the wind peeled back the top bill on one of the bundles, he saw that only the two bills on the outside of each bundle were hundreds. The rest were ones. It was real money, the whole heap of it, maybe $12,000, but it was less than a hundredth of the first-place prize. In poker, he was thinking with a smile, things are not as they appear.

✳

ISAAC WAS CONFIDENT, if not cocky. Ryan looked worried, but under the pressure of his disadvantage in the first hand Ryan bluffed and won.

In the next few hands, something interesting happened, and by interesting I mean, for me, excruciating. When I watch the video online still, five years after the game, it is excruciating.

While the sun went down behind big thunderheads, the dealer was not sailing the cards in air across the table, as he would have done inside. Under the lights for the TV cameras, on the windblown veranda, he was sliding each card carefully under his right hand to the player's hand.

In the second hand, Ryan, who was acting first, held the ace and the seven of hearts. A suited ace is strong enough to win three out of five times against random opposition. So, Ryan, with Ah7h, raised in the first round of betting to five hundred thousand chips, a raise of three hundred thousand over the blind bet required of him before the cards were dealt. This five hundred thousand ($17,500, as I cannot help but figure, in real American money) was an eighth of Ryan's stack, and his cards justified this investment.

Isaac, with a much weaker hand, called Ryan's bet. The bet was a twenty-seventh of Isaac's stack, and his cards, the 10d7d, also justified his investment, which was proportionately less. Isaac's bet was correct, in part, because his hand had an almost even chance against random opposition.

Each player's sense of the numbers and of the other's reading of the numbers is fundamental in the way that the dimensions of the strike zone, as reckoned by a particular umpire, are fundamental to the choices of the pitcher and the hitter.

The flop came 6h3h8d. Ryan unpaired, with an ace high, had a draw for the best hand possible on this board, the ace-high flush in hearts. To get two hearts on the flop, for Ryan, had been a ten-to-one shot. He knew that his hand as it now stood was strong in its potential, even if Isaac had made a pair. But the chance of Isaac's having a pair was only one in three. It was more probable that Ryan was ahead already, with substantially better odds for improvement. Ryan's chances of drawing the best possible hand, at this point, were one in three. Isaac's chances of drawing the best possible hand were almost certainly smaller. All things considered, Ryan saw these three cards as a very favorable flop.

Isaac was acting first after the flop. It was likely, he figured, that Ryan's hand was the stronger of the two at the moment. Most hands after the flop beat T-7 unpaired. Still, Isaac had four cards to a straight (6-7-8-T). This meant that any of the four nines was likely to give Isaac the winning hand. Any ten, on the turn or the river, pairing Isaac with the top card on the board, would be a probable winner. A seven, which would give Isaac a pair higher than two of the three cards flopped, was also strong. The diamond flush would come through one in twenty times, a remote chance which figures into the calculation in a case like this, where the odds are hovering near those of a coin flip. Without knowing Ryan's hand, Isaac correctly saw this board as favorable for his own hand, even though he had no pair and his high card was not strong. After this flop, Isaac would win two out of five hands against random opposition.

By betting all his chips, Isaac might induce Ryan to fold an unpromising hand. A hand that has not yet paired after the flop will be paired by the turn or river only one out of four times. Isaac knew that

Ryan's betting did not necessarily indicate the strength of his hand. Ryan, on the button now, might have bet on the strength of position alone. The similarity, by the way, in Ryan's pattern of play for these two hands with radically different cards, in different position, is precisely the kind of deception that game theory dictates. The pattern of betting disguises the content of Ryan's hand, while applying pressure on the opposition. Both Ryan and Isaac knew game theory, and each knew that the other knew.

To go all-in with T-7 unpaired may look foolhardy. But if the chance that Ryan would fold in response was greater than one in ten, Isaac could figure that his odds of winning the hand after betting, against random opposition, including the luck of the draw and the chance of a fold, were better than even. A better-than-even chance to win is a good betting position. On the basis of an analysis along these lines, Isaac went all-in.

Ryan's chances of winning against random opposition were better than two to one, much better than Isaac's, although neither Ryan nor Isaac knew this. Against any made pair, his chances would be less than even. His chances against someone with a hand that justifies betting everything might be less again, perhaps much less. If Ryan folded, however, and lost the $17,500 he had already committed to the pot, that loss was a certainty.

He called (for all his chips, $160,000) with visible resignation, because he calculated that risking everything was the move supported by probability. Since all his money was in the pot and there was no more betting to come, there was no reason to keep a poker face, and the resignation in his body language and in his facial expression looked to Isaac like good news.

Isaac jumped to his feet. The tournament was at stake. When he saw the A-7 of hearts, the high card was not a surprise. Isaac might well expect Ryan to have high card, even after he saw the resignation behind Ryan's call. Any hand that supported a call was likely to be ahead of an unpaired ten high. But Ryan's seven of hearts was much worse than another unpaired high card or a pair lower than seven would have been. The combination of the high card, the flush draw, and the seven eliminated five of the ten cards Isaac had counted among probable winners. Isaac's calculation of his chances went from almost even to a long shot, from better than two in five to only one in six. Even if Isaac paired his ten on the turn, he would still have to fade hearts on the river.

To fade a card in poker is to avoid a draw that would give the opponent a winning hand. The verb *fade* seems to have been lifted from the slang of dice and pool. In pool the power to fade the opposition requires superior skill. At the poker table, to fade the draw, as in dice to fade the odds, is a question of luck, but *fade* in this construction seems to imply that the winner has a magical power to generate luck by fading certain probabilities out of existence. To the mind of an aging poet, the phrase *fading hearts on the river* suggests more than merely avoiding hearts on the final card. *Fading hearts on the river* suggests heart-weariness on the journey for all of us, whether we call ourselves gamblers or not.

Now that the poker faces were taking a rest, Isaac summed up the sense of his position with one heart-weary syllable, "Yech!" followed by an uncool grimace, with his tongue stuck out of the left corner of his mouth. After a five came on the turn, Isaac could avoid disaster with a non-heart ten, nine, or four. It was not a hopeless situation. Isaac

had improved and was now what they call a four-to-one dog, short
for underdog. In other words, he would lose four out of five times in
this situation. When he did lose ($160,000 in real money, according to
my method of miscalculation, all four years of his college tuition), he
found himself behind in the chip count for the first time in several days.
He slumped, shrugged, and said, "Good hand."

If this was not yet the excruciating part, it looked bad enough.
Isaac's body language at this moment changed. His head, with his long
hair blowing, drooped. He worked the muscles of his face, as if to find
an expression that did not reveal his vulnerability. He failed. I have
read that some of the pain centers which respond to physical pain also
respond to this kind of disappointment. Isaac looked as if the wave
of good luck he had been riding steadily since the first day suddenly
broke, dragged him under, slammed him hard into the bottom, and
dropped him here at tableside trying to catch his breath.

His play had been, mathematically, as sound as Ryan's. The difference was luck. He could be satisfied, at least, with that, but this was
not much consolation. Zoe, Francie, Lillie, and Miriam were standing
together, looking as stunned as if Isaac had been physically hurt.

Ryan's demeanor shifted now from cagy defense to a more busi-
nesslike alertness. Momentum is an illusion in a game of cards, but the
momentum was with Ryan.

To follow what happened a few hands later, you have to bear in
mind that a serious player cannot bet consistently on the strength of
the cards he happens to have been dealt. To bet entirely on the pro-
portional strength of the hands lets other players know exactly where
things stand. This knowledge is a decisive advantage. The more profit-
able play is to reveal less about the cards, by betting less consistently

on the strength of the cards and more on an understanding of the opponent's pattern of betting.

Each player bets to represent a range of hands, and the choice of what to represent may be very loosely related to the actual cards. Both players know that the representations are false much of the time, because the bettor's aim is to deceive the opponent in ways that induce miscalculations. Every miscalculation on one side is good for the other side.

For most serious players, the bets in sequence are designed to suggest, after the deal, the flop, the turn, and the river, a plausible narrative about the shifting value of the cards in the bettor's hand. This narrative may be designed to persuade the opponent to fold in the mistaken belief that a weak hand is strong, or to raise in the belief that a strong hand is weak.

For a small percentage of players, the extreme nerds like Ryan and Isaac, the dance of misrepresentation involves mathematical logic developed in the study of game theory, a branch of mathematics made famous in the film *A Beautiful Mind*. According to game theory, each player should randomize his representations in a way that makes it impossible for the opponent to gain an advantage by skill. Because Ryan and Isaac each saw the other as a worthy opponent, game theory offered the most effective pattern of play, including the pattern of misrepresentations. Each player's job, given the likelihood of misrepresentation, was to read precisely how each bet represented his opponent's hand and to interpret this, given the history of the opponent's betting, by observing every detail of the opponent's behavior at that moment.

When Ryan raised to five hundred thousand chips ($16,000) before the flop in the next hand in question, the same raise he had made in both of the hands previously mentioned, Isaac saw weakness in Ryan's face and in the deliberateness of his body language. Ryan was trying to exploit the momentum of having pulled ahead, despite holding unimpressive cards. Isaac believed, correctly, that the bet felt high to Ryan in proportion to the quality of his hand. Regardless of the cards Isaac happened to be holding (the abysmally low 7c3c, as he now saw), the correct play in response was to force Ryan to choose, either to risk his tournament life or to fold a hand that he already felt uneasy about betting.

Isaac, although relatively sure that he himself held the weaker of the two hands, raised the bet to 1.75 million ($62,000), and Ryan looked even more distressed. This look confirmed that Isaac's play was correct. In other words, a player of Ryan's disposition, holding the cards that Ryan actually held, would fold most of the time in response to this bet. To call would force Ryan, eventually, to bet most of his stack on cards for which a raise to five hundred thousand chips had felt risky.

This is the excruciating part. Often, an inexperienced player, when he bluffs, feels uncomfortable about his exposure to risk and he tries, reflexively, with his facial expression and body language to intimidate his opponent, to discourage the call or raise. The reflexive effort to intimidate is a tell, which most strong players can easily read.

After a little experience, players on a bluff, wanting to avoid that tell, often try to look as unintimidating as they can, as if their cards are so good that they really want the opponent to stay in the hand. These slightly more experienced players may give an intimidating stare when they have a winning hand. If this intimidating stare reads as the tell for a bluff, the opponent is more likely to call. But the tactics of reversal also may be tells, when the body language appears staged rather than reflexive.

Mind games, based on what each player thinks the other thinks he thinks, reverse and re-reverse their logic endlessly. Isaac and Ryan both were aware of this and were trying to read each other's body language at the table, to discriminate between inadvertent tells and deliberate false tells.

Isaac, after announcing a raise of more than $40,000, looked down while he was moving his chips, as I described earlier, so that his windblown hair completely covered his face. Ryan was staring, searching for a sign, and the commentator read the look on Ryan's face as saying, "How can I read this guy when I can't even see him with the hair? It's like trying to call down Cousin Itt."

Then, as a triple-reverse mind game, Isaac gave Ryan an aggressive look. Isaac's thinking about this look was complicated. He thought that Ryan would read it correctly as a deliberate ploy and not as the reflexive intimidation of the unsophisticated player, because, in fact, it really was a deliberate ploy. The fact that it was a ploy and not a reflexive action, Isaac hoped, would make him look like a slightly more sophisticated player with a strong hand reversing the reflex, to induce a call. When Ryan saw the look, however, his expression as I read it now on the video shifted, subtly but definitively, from a searching gaze to a look of understanding.

I have watched this moment many times, and I cannot isolate how Ryan's face expresses the change in his thinking. But it does. Something happens around the eyes and mouth. Maybe there is an infinitesimal change in the tilt of his head, a slight dilation of the pupils. The commentator seeing this as well said, "He's gonna play. He's gonna play this one."

Even though he had no pair, only a Q-9, without a promising draw, not much better than average cards, Ryan said, "I'm all-in," and he looked confident. Isaac, whose weakness Ryan had read, despite the dark glasses, now saw Ryan's bare-faced confidence and was forced to fold his pathetic 7c3c rather than commit another $250,000 and risk his survival in the tournament. Now Isaac found himself at a two-to-one disadvantage in chips.

There's one more hand I want to describe. This one comes a little later. Ryan with a 7c5s calls the blind, and Isaac with a 2d3d checks. The flop comes Qh4hAc. Isaac checks, and Ryan bets three hundred thousand, although he has a weak hand, because a bet, especially after a check on the flop, will induce a fold a large percentage of the time. This is what makes the button such an advantageous position. Even if Isaac does not fold, his answering bet and body language may give Ryan information worth the price of a bet. Isaac sees that a five will give him a straight, but knows that the odds against a five are six to one. Still, since Ryan's bet in his position does not necessarily indicate any particular strength, Isaac calls. This call probably indicates that Isaac does not have an ace, because it is usually best to protect the top pair from further draws by making a raise. Most of the time, a call in this situation simply indicates that Isaac is protecting whatever hand he has against the standard continuation bet.

When the turn comes Kd, which is no help to either player, Isaac checks and Ryan checks behind. This confirms the probability that Ryan's continuation bet did not indicate strength. The river is Qc, pairing the queen on the board. Neither player has reason to believe that his own pitifully low hand will beat the other. But there is reason on both sides to bet, to represent, for example, making three queens after staying in with second pair, or holding the high straight, after setting a trap by checking on the turn. A big bet makes the board, what they call a coordinated board (AKQQ4), look scary, even for an opponent with a pocket pair or a king. Neither Isaac nor Ryan by now thinks that the other has anything. Both think that the other will be likely to fold, if it seems that his opponent has so much as a jack or a ten high, which are the best unpaired hands.

Ryan knows for certain that his seven high will be the winning hand in this situation fewer than one in ten times, and Isaac has the very worst hand possible. The term for Isaac's hand, in a game where the lowest possible hand wins, is the nut low. In this game, of course, the lowest possible hand does not win.

Still, Isaac opens with a bet of seven hundred thousand, having had no indication of strength from Ryan. It seems probable that Ryan will fold in response. Ryan thinks this over. He has one of the very worst hands possible, with no reason to believe that Isaac's hand is weaker than his own, but very deliberately, he raises to two million ($70,000). He must sense weakness. This is what they call a sick raise.

After the game, Isaac learned that one of Ryan's friends, who had played at Isaac's table earlier in the tournament, saw Isaac stare at his opponent only when he bluffed. Isaac's thinking about this look had yielded good results until the last few hands, but he did not realize that he had been tellingly consistent in his use of this tactic. Ryan's knowledge of the tell, as it turned out, may have been decisive in their contest for first place. It is easy to see now on the video that, just after Isaac stares at Ryan, in both these hands, Ryan chooses to raise.

Two million, at this point, is almost a third of Isaac's remaining stack. At first, as I read his expression, Isaac is puzzled. He has made his bet with a strong conviction that Ryan is on a bluff. The raise in response makes no sense to him. To see Isaac respond with such palpable disbelief must make Ryan feel very uneasy. Isaac puts his head facedown on his arms. He cannot call, because he knows his own cards cannot win. One commentator says, "It's like Isaac's cards are turned up on the board, the way Ryan is playing him." The other says about Isaac, "He's got the worst two cards you can have at this moment."

When Isaac raises his head, he looks at Ryan again. Ryan still looks nervous, like a player on a bluff. Then, Isaac stares off into the distance for a long time, going through the sequence of betting to settle in his mind what Ryan might be holding and to let Ryan see him thinking it through. Finally, he says, "Raise. All-in." He bets all his chips (about $234,000 more), because he still believes that Ryan is bluffing, and the only way Isaac can possibly win the hand is for Ryan to fold his bluff against Isaac's even bigger bluff. Ryan, a few hands ago, read Isaac's bluff correctly and pulled ahead in the match. He seems to have read Isaac's earlier bluff in this hand too. If he calls this last and sickest bluff, he wins the tournament.

Isaac is betting that Ryan, if he is truly as uncertain about his own bluff as he appears, will conclude that he cannot call. Isaac feels that he has constructed a plausible narrative about his hand. If Isaac hit the flop, he might have called Ryan's small bet and checked the turn to induce a bluff on the river. This would make perfect sense of Isaac's bet and his raise all-in. If this narrative were Ryan's sense of Isaac's play, Ryan might fold a relatively strong hand. But Isaac does not believe that Ryan's hand is strong.

Ryan knows, in fact, that nine out of ten hands, bluff or not, will beat his own, and he folds, again with correct mathematical logic.

To do otherwise would be foolish. Isaac, although he could muck his cards face-down as usual, throws the 2-3 onto the board face-up, to rattle Ryan with the knowledge of having been beaten by a hand that could not win against any other hand.

Ryan smiles and says, "You're gonna like when that's on TV." You have to like Ryan, as well, for being a good sport after such a setback.

Isaac looks surprised. He asks, "Did you drop a queen?"

Ryan shakes his head. "I bluff-raised."

"I was pretty sure you had."

After this hand the two of them are even in chips, and Isaac savors his miraculous return from the brink. But the seesawing, as it turns out, is over. Ryan wins two more big hands, neither of which involves a bluff, and Isaac, who seemed to have the whole tournament in the bag, wins second place.

❋

IN HER LAST two hours at the rail, with Isaac playing for $670,000 of real money, betting millions of chips on every hand, Zoe could not seem to catch her breath. She wanted to make a good impression on Isaac's mother, who had just arrived and who stood beside her. But what she really needed at that moment was to be away from the game, where she could sit calmly, close her eyes, and breathe.

Night was falling. The wind was blowing hard, and she was freezing in her sundress. She took deep breaths. She could feel air going in. Her lungs were full, and still her blood was screaming to her brain for oxygen. Her heart was pounding in her chest and in her ears.

In the final stage of this distress, to watch Ryan, a stranger and an upstart, steal from Isaac the first prize, which had been at Isaac's fingertips for three days, was too much. This was evil. Zoe hated Ryan. But she saw Isaac taking in what happened with a shrug, and she loved that shrug. She loved the friendly way he smiled when he shook Ryan's hand. First place would have made him happier, but cash like this, so early in a tournament career, was gravy.

The night before, an interviewer had asked Isaac which was more important, the money or the tournament title. Isaac replied, if he were given a choice between, on the one hand, winning first place and everybody knowing that he won, but without getting the money, or, on the other hand, winning the money, with nobody ever knowing he had won a thing, he would take the money every time. It made him laugh to consider the alternative.

Now Zoe watched him move around the table, calm and cheerful, and she found it difficult to feel disappointed for him. He was feeling happy for himself. An unbelievably large sum of money was his. Francie felt as puzzled and disarmed by Isaac's cheer as Zoe was.

These last two days, which had been putting Zoe through the wringer, were pure oxygen in Isaac's blood and brain. For their last moment on camera, the commentators, Isaac, and Ryan lined up and toasted each other with bottles of the sponsor's beer, not great beer. While the others took a polite sip, Isaac started celebrating in good earnest with a gulp. This, he had no doubt now, was the life.

But poker, I keep thinking, is deceptive. Everything always is at risk. The game and the prize money, my wife and our three children, with Zoe, who was becoming part of the family now—all of them at the moment were in the Devil's Triangle.

THE MOOM

in light of which
a BOY and GIRL
transfixed
by MYSTERIES are drawn
into the celebration of the MIND
at *PLAY*

ONE CLEAR AFTERNOON in mid-September, just past Isaac's first birthday, I took him for a stroll. The sun was low and the ghost of a moon hung over the treetops east. Leaves were beginning to turn. Without expecting Isaac to understand, I leaned down to the stroller, pointed into the sky, and said softly, "Moon."

He looked up, held out his tiny right hand in the same direction, took a long, throaty gasp, and said nothing. He was not yet speaking. He could not walk. Very little of his hair and few of his teeth had yet come in. He was precocious, as far as anyone could tell, in no respect. But it was clear that he had seen the moon, he knew that it was being pointed out to him, and he was transfixed. "Moon," I kept saying, "moon," and Isaac looked up, steadily, with palpable amazement, and repeated gasps.

When I think of him twenty years later as a poker shark on a sick bluff, face hidden by long hair and shades, I find it odd how far this transformation had already come to pass by the time he was four. At four he was cultivating his knack for games. He surprised us all, eventually, by choosing a game as his career. For me, the world of high-stakes poker will always be a foreign realm. I hope, by writing my way into it here, to understand my son. But first, like Isaac as a child, I need a running start.

A few weeks before Isaac's stroll, Francie and I had been in the kitchen, getting supper ready, while Isaac was crawling around the bare wooden floor in nothing but his diaper, looking for something to amuse himself. His occasional *ma* or *ba* or *da* had no consistent relation to anything, as far as we could tell. But the lack of evidence that Isaac was at all precocious made no difference in our estimation of his gifts.

Francie was speculating about how much Isaac understood, and on a whim, I did something neither of us had done before. "Isaac," I said, in a normal speaking voice, because I disliked baby talk, "go into the living room, get your ball, and bring it back in here. All right?"

I said this without gestures, but Isaac did not pause to consider. He immediately crawled out the kitchen door, down the hall, turned left into the living room, and came crawling straight back, pushing the ball in front of him, without further prompting. You may be thinking that a cocker spaniel can understand when someone says to fetch a ball. If you are thinking this way, you are missing the point. The point is, Isaac was a genius, and this proved it.

At the supermarket a few weeks later, they were giving away helium balloons, the ones made from two pieces of foil glued at the seam. I brought one home. In the stairwell on the way up into the apartment, the sound of Isaac's gobbledygook was an elixir to the fatherly heart.

I walked into the living room, where he and Francie were playing together on the floor. Getting down on my hands and knees, I held out the balloon, eye level, for Isaac to see. He watched, with anticipation. I released the string, and the balloon floated up and bounced into the ceiling. I expected him to be delighted. He was not delighted. He screamed as though someone had unleashed a banshee in the room.

I wished so much that I could read his mind, I believed that I could. If the moon was a deific ball in a heavenly procession, the balloon, in Isaac's mind, must be a demonic ball misplaced in this world, yearning to escape again into the sky. Its unnatural impulse made it an atrocity. For several months, Isaac could not look at any helium balloon without screaming in terror.

Still, whenever we pointed out the moon, Isaac stared at it, euphoric. Later, when he reared up on his hind legs, and started to cruise around the apartment on two feet, he would sometimes find that the moon was outside, and he would stand at the window looking up and saying its name, "Moon! Noom! Moom!" He started talking quite a bit and understanding more. The world was overflowing with amazements.

Soon he was delighted, once a week, to ride on my shoulders to the curb when the garbage truck was passing. Francie drew a garbage truck in icing on the cake for his second birthday, and he loved it.

❋

EARLY IN 2013, in his ninth year of serious play, Isaac's poker winnings ran unusually high. In a Monte Carlo cash game, he won a single pot of more than a million euro. A few months later, at the warm-up for the high roller in Macau, he made 2.579 million Hong Kong dollars for finishing second in a world-class field, and he won four times that much for finishing fifth in the main event which started the following day. Hong Kong dollars make this sound like more than it was. In American money, the combined winnings from Monte Carlo and Macau were about $2 million. Meanwhile, online, in the high-stakes cash games, he was on a heater, one of the top few winners in the world.

I might as well confess, however, since my disposition has helped make my grown son what he is, and since my telling makes this story what it is. Regardless of the ambient excitement, I am a sad sack, from a line of sad sacks, Jews and Presbyterians alike.

My great-great-great-great-grandfather, Samuel Brooks, for whom I am named, was the first American mayor of the town of Natchez, Mississippi. On a certain night two hundred years ago, he was expected by custom to escort his two daughters to their first formal ball. That evening, after they had dressed, the girls came down to the parlor to show off their new gowns, which their parents admired.

Finally, my namesake said, "Now, young ladies, go upstairs. Take off your ball gowns and go to bed. You must learn to bear disappointment." This only begins to suggest the depths of my gene pool.

In her off hours, Francie as a psychiatrist has used the term *dysthymia* for my mind-set. After referring to the diagnostic criteria, I disagree. I think of my sadness as a poetic disposition. I prefer the labels *melancholy, dejection,* or even, to exaggerate my tendency, *despair.* For my usual mood, I might use John Crowe Ransom's phrase *brown study,* though he used that label to indicate the mood of the corpse at a viewing, and I am not quite that far gone.

I am not a victim of Churchill's *black dog* or of Tennessee Williams's *blue devil.* I am not hounded or possessed, although my mood does hit its lows. Some of my friends' moods, unlike mine, have dropped into psychosis. Some have killed themselves, and others tried. As I imagine such abysses, where I have never gone, they make the shoals of my moods look inviting. Silly as I feel to say so, in the sea of sadness, I live, like the American flounder, near the beach.

This fish, which some call the sole, starts out as a typical species. While he matures, he gravitates to the bottom, and he finds that his left eye migrates slowly to the right side of his head. The left half of the body goes white, like the belly of a catfish. This is not a badge of honor, or a source of shame. It is the nature of the species. The mature flounder is a bottom-dweller. His right side, which becomes his back, is mottled camouflage.

My own soul may appear misshapen, though it has evolved effectively for bottom-dwelling. I thrive in sadness as a natural habitat where I know the richness of the world, receptive to both joy and pain. Clinical depression is another realm, and I have tried to imagine it as well as I can, but I would not wish for anyone to know it from inside.

I am grateful to sleep without medication, to have a steady appetite, to enjoy my work as a teacher, my students, and my colleagues. Even though I cannot experience these pleasures as steadily as I sometimes wish, my time with my family is precious to me, and I sustain a high level of concerted attention to my work, which I find gratifying. For all of this, I thank the gods, without believing any god in heaven cares about me in the least.

❋

WHEN ISAAC BEGAN to talk, not especially early, there was nothing noteworthy about his speech. But Francie and I soon found some of what he said a little odd. In the car one day, when he was not yet two, he was in the back in his car seat, and I asked him over one shoulder what that sound was. He said, "That was gas, muffled by my diaper."

I could not think where he had learned the word *muffled*. But his use of it in this sentence was his own contraption. What was truly strange was his ability to generate new thinking. Not long after the gas-muffling incident, he was sitting in his high chair in the kitchen, enjoying one of his favorite foods, breast of chicken, which I had cut up for him into little pieces, so he could handle it, with his few teeth.

"Dad," he asked, "where does chicken come from?"

"Poultry farms," I said. The boy loved words, but he seemed to sense that I was using the word *poultry* to distract him, to avoid the topic that had begun to form in his mind.

He said, "What does this"—he held up a morsel—"have to do with chickens, like chickens on the farm?"

Precociousness, I thought, is not all fun. Coming at the question straight seemed the best way to avoid making the answer look like a problem. "It *is* the chicken."

Isaac said, "How do you get it from the chicken?"

At that age he loved vehicles, the bigger the better, so I tried emphasizing transport as a further distraction, while busily rearranging things in the cupboard. "Well, they raise the chickens on the farm, and when they get them ready for the store, they bring them there in a *huge* refrigerator truck from really far away."

"But how do they get *this* from the chicken?" He held up that little slice of his favorite dish. He was going to find out what I was not telling him, or know the reason why.

I said, again, "It *is* the chicken. Farmers raise the chickens for people like us to eat." Opening the refrigerator and looking in, I was dimly aware that I was looking for help, and that there was none on the shelves in the refrigerator.

"But what do they do with the *chickens*?"

After I moved a few things on the shelves, Isaac asked me again, "How do they get this from the chicken?" He was not giving up. He knew. He just needed confirmation.

As a last-ditch effort, I put the gruesome part into an adverbial clause at the beginning of a long, compound, complex sentence, with more interesting things in the last part. "After they kill them and put them into packages, they take them on the big refrigerator truck to the store, and when we go, you ride in the seat high up in the cart, remember?—and we buy the uncooked chicken, and bring it home for me to cook, the way you like it, with potatoes for hash browns . . . and ice cream for dessert." Seeing that my syntax was not up to the job, I quickly made the bribe explicit. "You want some ice cream?" We seldom gave him any sweets.

"They kill them?"

"Yes." The offer of ice cream, suddenly, felt shameful.

"That's not very nice."

Isaac at two wanted nothing more to do with chicken. Ice cream would be fine, thank you very much, but as for chicken, he did not take another bite, although Francie and I kept eating it, and he never expected us to stop.

He was a vegetarian, for several years.

At two, he was paying attention to everything. His brain was set, in every single cortical area, for every waking second, on Record. He could say which turns to take on the way to his friend Jake's house or to the park. He noticed when a picture changed in the waiting room at the doctor's office. That spring, when I took him on walks at the nature center, I brought along my field guide, to learn the names of wildflowers. I would crouch by a flower, show him the picture in the book, and say the name, not because there was any reason for him to learn such things, but because I wanted to learn them, and I was trying to make this an entertainment for him as well. But soon I noticed that he was learning the wildflowers faster than I was.

The summer before we moved into the apartment on the grounds of the psychiatric hospital where Francie did her residency, at Cornell's

Westchester Division in White Plains, we went there to visit her friend from school who was already a resident. We had a picnic with him in the garden and went for a walk. Isaac and Greg were talking together while they walked, and Isaac pointed out the chicory and smartweed. Greg asked about a few more flowers growing wild along the sidewalk, and Isaac knew their names as well. He was not yet three, and his taxonomic skill struck Greg, who had studied developmental psychology, but not wildflowers, as bizarre.

※

ISAAC AND I spent a great deal of our time together playing games. But I swear, before he reached the age of three, I never took him into the casino. His mother and I tried walking him through the front door of a Mississippi riverboat, where we introduced him, at three, to the slot machine, but he has always disliked slot machines, because of the terrible odds, and, in any case, they kicked us out for bringing him. It was just as well. He was happier feeding ducks on the levee.

※

THAT WAS WHEN Isaac began to develop superpowers. As Super Isaac, he could fly in outer space. His mother gave him a cape. He had x-ray vision and superhuman strength, which made him very dangerous in a fight. Sometimes he was called upon to rescue his imaginary friends, Clock and Guggenheimer, though sometimes they had superpowers too, and the three of them would fight bad guys together. In our neighborhood, even inside the house, there were countless bad guys, and dinosaurs ran amok. Allosaurs and tyrannosaurs were a particular problem. Isaac, Clock, and Guggenheimer kept things under control.

At this same age, Isaac began to wake up screaming and crying from his nightmares, sometimes more than once a week. He was too upset ever to tell us what he dreamed, but it seemed to be a single recurrent dream. He would scream, from deep in a trance, thrashing with his hands, as if he were trying to brush away something at his chest and belly—this same gesture every time. He was thrashing for his life.

To comfort him we had to wake him from the dream, which seemed to have him in its power like an evil spell. I would speak to him in a loud, clear voice about where we were in the house and what we were doing. He kept screaming. I turned on lights and lifted him into a standing position, took him to the sink, ran cool water, and put his hand in it. As soon as he could stand, we walked around the house until he came to understand that the dream was not happening here in the waking world, and he was safe. Then he would come to sleep, still sobbing, between us in our bed. He never had the bad dream more than once in a single night.

I suspected that his dream involved the dinosaurs which obsessed him during the day. His frantic hands were fending off the dinosaurs' attacking claws.

❋

E. O. WILSON and Steven Pinker, writers I find wonderfully intelligent, have written that the interpretation of dreams is superstitious garbage. Random neuronal activity during sleep, according to their view, generates a play of insignificant illusion. The chaos in the mind of a sleeper is something like psychosis, they have asserted, and the less highly we regard that crazy stuff, the better off we are. I disagree.

My mother, whose pen name is Ellen Douglas, was a first-rate novelist and writer of nonfiction. She wrote a book called *Truth*, which contains, among other things, the story about my namesake, Samuel Brooks. I was raised by her to believe that telling stories is often as close as people come to truth. The art of telling stories, as I learned it at her knee, in fiction and nonfiction, is to tell true lies. Doing this, by her lights and by mine, is good. Dreaming is similarly good, and true, and intellectual analysis is one of many kinds of waking dreams worth having.

When I tell dreams, even my own, let alone Isaac's, I am like everyone else, utterly unreliable. But I get truly obnoxious when I start to analyze them. The simple fact that people lie when they tell stories does not make far-fetched intellectual contraptions any less offensive.

Intellectuals are obnoxious because they play their mind games ostentatiously, and everyone agrees that there is more to life than games. The problem is, some people cannot help themselves. They like games. Anyone who distrusts abstractions has my blessing. I do too. I suggest you skip offending passages, like the next three paragraphs, which justify my understanding of night terrors.

Freud wrote that our discomfort with the truths revealed in dreams can make us anxious to deny their substance. The more ardently we deny the truth, he said, the more clearly we reveal our sense that we have seen the truth in what we wish to deny.

Wilson and Pinker find Freud's writing about denial brilliant for the way he uses paradox to place the opposing argument at a logical impasse. Freud's logic, they say, is a tour de force of rhetoric, the original Catch-22. But if dreams really are nonsense, they remind us, it is merely truthful to say that they are and to take Freud with a grain of salt.

On this point they make sense. But their assumption about the craziness of the sleeping brain is no more logical than to assume the reality of Freud's hidden truth. In fact, it seems extravagant to assume that a brain, evolved to represent relationships between organisms and the world in which they seek survival, would waste such a large part of its energies on superfluous illusions. The logic following from the craziness assumption, moreover, is tautology: if dreams are nonsense, it makes sense to say that dreams are nonsense. This apparent impasse in tautology, the authors ask us to believe, refutes the impasse in Freud's paradox. Among scientists, as among poets, there is rhetoric enough to go around.

For those who cannot see both the absurdity and the truth in dreams, or in the newspaper, for that matter, I recommend the clarity of calm attention to the breath.

❋

ISAAC'S NIGHT TERRORS, apart from rhetoric, concerned me, because he was suffering from them. Few things are more intolerable to a parent than to stand by, helpless, while a child is suffering. Something in Isaac made this dream recur, I thought, something that frightened him in his waking life.

Dinosaurs mattered to him because they were so big and powerful and strange. When they came to life in his imagination, he was the seat of their power. The power was intoxicating. When he was awake, he could use his superpowers to respond. But what was I supposed to do for him in his dreams, when he needed help and no one else could be there for him?

One day, I spent a long time with Isaac drawing a tea party for dinosaurs. On a huge piece of brown packaging paper we drew allosaurs and tyrannosaurs sitting on little chairs, with hind legs politely crossed at the knee, holding teacups and saucers in their foreclaws. There were little cakes and cookies on the table. Isaac and I drew. We laughed. We fantasized to our hearts' content. When the dinosaurs talked, they sounded British, and frightfully upper-crust. No one knows precisely how they developed these accents in Montana and in Colorado where they lived, but one hoped that their way of speaking and behaving might indicate that they had learned to be more sociable.

Maybe the conversation over tea and biscuits influenced Isaac's choice to be a dinosaur at Halloween, when he was three. He chose to be an iguanodon, a species which he liked for several reasons. It was not the Lizard King, as Isaac would be dubbed by poker commentators, but it was big, with something like the shape and posture of a tyrannosaur. On each foreclaw, it had an unusual kind of horn, which resembled a thumb and which the animal could supposedly use as an effective weapon against predators. It was important for Isaac to specify that he was an iguanodon, because that species was, like him, herbivorous. Isaac learned about iguanodons when we were looking at the pictures in library books, and he remembered the details and gave them as his reasons for the choice. For Halloween, his mother smeared him with green makeup, and he wore green clothes. He held his thumbs up stiff, and lumbered from house to house. I told the ladies at each door, please, not to be frightened. He *was* a dinosaur, but he was vegetarian. Isaac found this very gratifying.

❋

ONE OF ISAAC'S favorite fantasy games at three was the Alien Game. He would play this game with Francie and me for as long as we could stand it. It was a role-playing game. One person was the alien, and the other person interviewed the alien. What do you eat on your planet? Do you cook? Where do you live? Are there animals there? Is there water? What does the sky look like? Do you play games? How do you make music? Do you have dreams?

Isaac liked to play the Alien Game when he was in the tub or when one of us was in the tub, so the scenario he made up in the following story, which Francie transcribed while he was telling it, fits that context. "An alien spaceship took off at midnight and was flying for days and days. One day it landed in a boy's front yard. The alien came in the kitchen door and said, 'Is it time for my bath yet? Just fill the bath with bright fuzzy and with warm fizzy Coke. The fizz takes my dirt off, but it leaves my slime alone.'"

The alien in this story, who had green peacock feathers and thirteen red eyes, wanted to eat in the tub—potato latkes with mustard and Pickapeppa sauce. Then, he wanted to be thrown into the clothes dryer to get warm and dry for bed, where he would sing a lullaby in his own language, "Thgin, thgin."

The Alien Game was fantasy in a loose format, without an objective. But Isaac at three also began to take an interest in more formalized games. He learned the recipe format from keeping Francie and me company while we cooked. Impressed with the power of a recipe to make the grownups do exactly what it said, Isaac began to form recipes of his own, with the most ridiculous and disgusting ingredients he could imagine.

Poems also had a formal rhetoric which he found appealing. Isaac sometimes dictated poems to me, and a few of these survive. Here's one called "Doomsday," to which he gave an explanatory subtitle, "It's not till the end of the next month." This may be read as a clue to the mysteries of the moon, the balloons, and the night terrors. He made this up when he was four.

The day the earth explodes
The trees go shooting up like rocket ships,
The ground falls down like a dead person,
And, as the ground falls out, it flips upside down.
The sky is the beginning of space.
You'll probably see trees floating around up in it,
like rocket ships or planes.
The oceans will fall out of the planet;
The mountains go shooting up, upside down, like rocket ships.
There's a lot more that happens on doomsday,
But most of it's not very interesting.
The pitchers usually get cracks in them.

❋

IN THE SUMMER of 2013, after his winning streak in the earlier part of the year, Isaac was playing online in a luxury hotel room in Vancouver when he lost well over a million dollars in two days. A few weeks later, he was down another half a million, and then more. His losses for that time were the greatest in the online game from anybody in the world. As Samuel Brooks, or anyone else with my dark disposition or with an understanding of probability, would tell you, we can expect extreme reversals in our luck from time to time.

❋

OUR ROOM ON the island of Saint Lucia was a thatched hut in the shade of palm trees just a few steps from a quiet beach. There was a bar on the beach, where we ate lunch. The water at our feet was incredibly clear, and the pristine little reef nearby was full of fishes, sponges, and corals. That trip, when Isaac was four, was the best vacation we had ever had.

We rented a jeep and drove miles inland into the rain forest on a trail along the bed of a stream, a trail rocky enough to keep me wondering what we would do if we broke an axle. We drove north on a two-lane blacktop hundreds of feet over the sea. Isaac and I kept teasing Francie about the drop. We drove south, through the town of Soufrière, and on one of the two volcanoes under the tropical sun, we saw and smelled the sulfurous hot springs and the fumaroles.

Every morning for breakfast, and every evening for dinner, we climbed a long wooden stair on the hillside to the balcony at our hotel. We looked out over a mile-wide bay with twin volcanoes on the opposite shore. The fruit they served was local bananas sweeter than I could have imagined, papayas, and mangoes. There were warm, freshly roasted local peanuts to go with our tropical drinks. There was that day's catch for dinner, and peanut ice cream for dessert.

Isaac loved it, even though he came down with the chicken pox. He always tended to run high fevers, and this time he topped 106 degrees. He needed ibuprofen, acetaminophen, a cool shower, and a dip in the sea. We gave him all these, one after another, two or three at a time. Luckily the worst of his fever was short-lived, and his headache and nausea were relatively mild. He understood what we told him, and he was careful not to scratch his hundreds of sores. Still, after the worst of the fever passed, he felt out of it, exhausted.

He had fun anyway. He lolled on the beach and drank fruit drinks. We played games, and he was happy. I carried him in my arms. He rode piggy-back up the 110 steps to the balcony for breakfast and for dinner. It would have been better if he were well, but I would not trade the memory of that little boy nestling in my arms, and laughing while he rode, for anything.

※

A FEW YEARS later Isaac, like his father at that age, began to feel an uncontrollable panic at the thought of his own death. I suspect this panic about the inconceivable might be related, like his doomsday poem, to night terrors and to the horror of helium balloons. In Isaac's mind, and in my own, this quandary seems to linger in brown studies.

During his senior year in high school, when he got more and more withdrawn, Francie and I worried that, like me, he might be what psychiatrists would call dysthymic. One of his classmates put together a series of video clips where students did things that revealed their character. A bully, for example, appeared on camera gleefully pelting one of his friends with a grapefruit. Isaac in his clip sat at a table in the cafeteria alone. The soundtrack played "Bridge over Troubled Water," while, unaware of the camera, Isaac, in a brown study, stared into the distance and drank his chocolate milk. His friends found this hilarious. So did he.

More recently, after trying various physical fitness regimens to improve his energy level and his mood, Isaac has found that a norepinephrine and dopamine reuptake inhibitor taken daily in a very small dose is effective. This may be placebo effect. But it works.

Zoe in eighth grade also sank into melancholy. Things went out of her control. She had always wanted to do ballet. At three, when she saw children dancing in Rossini's *Cinderella* at the Civic Opera House, she could not contain herself. She stood in her seat, pointed, and said, loudly, "I want to do that!" Then, because she would not stop insisting, her family arranged for lessons. She worked, hard at dance lessons, four days a week and more during the summer.

When Zoe was in sixth grade, Saturday afternoons at the dance studio were her favorite time. She loved rainy days, when the wood of the barre felt soft and gummy. You could scratch it off with your nail. The dressing room was filled with an atmosphere of rain in the city, mixed with a locker-room scent, and under that the smells of the warm leather of your slippers, the sap of the resin to keep your toes from slipping out from under you, talc, hairspray, and torn-open oranges, which the teacher said were a perfect food for dancers.

On the bench just after class, Zoe watched the teacher's favorite take off her shoes, wiggle her unwrapped toes, and smile. Inside her own toe shoes, Zoe knew from the usual pain, she would find her toes in their wrappings bloody and misshapen. Soon, she would have to quit the class. Her childhood body had been too slight to bend the rigid shank in the sole of the shoe. Her weight, on point, instead of resting partially on her heel, jammed into her toes, and now her adolescent body suddenly went wrong again and was not slight enough. Years later, she would have surgery on her right foot to repair the damage.

Giving up ballet made her impossibly sad. Her psychiatrist told her parents she was depressed. Later, she took up theater, and she was delighted to lose herself again in that.

※

WHEN HE WAS four, Isaac and I would sometimes search for lost golf balls in the woods around the five-hole course on the grounds of the hospital where we lived. We would choose a couple of sturdy fallen limbs with solid crooks at the end, a long one for me and a short one for him. With these as clubs, we worked our way, each of us with a ball, very slowly around the course. I found this style of play well suited to the insane asylum. Isaac, as club champion, inherited his great-grandfather's mantle, and he soon graduated to plastic and cast-metal children's clubs, when a set of these turned up at a garage sale for five bucks. He could not believe how fancy these were, compared with the fallen limbs.

Wiffle ball was another sport he liked. He threw Frisbees. He tried sword fights and javelin throwing, with swords and javelins made from stems of common reeds. He liked racing, tumbling, climbing, and all manner of athletics.

❋

PEOPLE WHO CLAIM not to care about winning usually present this attitude as virtuous. The Sherman Park League, where Isaac played baseball after third grade, was religious in its devotion to the noncompetitive spirit. This meant that all the children got a chance at bat and in the field. There were no benchwarmers. Everyone took turns fielding the various positions. Noncompetitive play was fun, theoretically, for the children who were not strong as athletes.

Isaac thought it was humiliating for the children who could not catch to keep missing the ball during their turns as catcher. He said that his teammates who could not throw strikes dreaded their turns as pitcher. It was useless for them to beg with the coach for a position where they would humiliate themselves less steadily, though many of them tried. The children were delivered up as human sacrifices to their parents' faith in noncompetitive baseball.

The year before he joined a team, Isaac had wanted to learn the mechanics of pitching. We got a video and watched together. Then, we worked on his technique in the backyard. We enjoyed this, though neither of us has much talent as an athlete. After a few weeks, although he did not have a pitcher's arm and could not throw especially fast, Isaac was throwing strikes most of the time, a skill which he soon discovered almost no one in the Sherman Park League thought of learning.

The noncompetitive faith dictated, however, that Isaac pitch no more than the incompetent. When the dad who was the coach started orienting the players in the field and accidentally placed the shortstop on the wrong side of second base, everyone on the team who had ever played or watched baseball could see the months of misery they would have to endure. Isaac told me he would like to join another league, but for this I would have had to drive across town and wait for him to finish practice, instead of dropping him off in the neighborhood and coming back when he was done. My fecklessness doomed him to Sherman Park.

On his rare turns pitching, he was more effective than his ball speed seemed to promise. He figured out which batters liked to swing at pitches in the dirt, and he threw them what they liked. The opposing coaches took a dim view of this attitude, but his teammates saw no problem.

The rule in the Sherman Park League was that no one would keep score, but children on both teams did keep score and taunted each other with the numbers, always. Coaches pretended not to care who won, but baseball is a competitive game. People are competitive creatures. Species evolve in competition between survivors and nonsurvivors. Everything alive competes.

❋

FOR THE MOMENT, despite the drawbacks at Sherman Park and the wonderful prizes in Macau, I would like to affirm the value of noncompetition.

Among those who are "trying to learn to use words," T. S. Eliot says in the second of his *Four Quartets*, "there is no competition." Eliot wrote this between spells as a volunteer air raid warden in London during the Blitz, when England seemed to be losing in its competition with the ultimate evil in the world.

Eliot's faith at that moment in the spirit of his art, his statement that there is no competition, for many readers since, including me, has been inspiring. But the statement would be superfluous if there really were no competition. Noncompetition is an inspiring model of behavior only insofar as it *competes*, heroically, with competition as the alternate model. In this contest, most of us suspect that competition will win.

Regardless of what Eliot says, we know that writers do compete, whether they celebrate this fact or not, for the limited attention of readers. Eliot competed well for his particular audience, and I respect him for this, just as I respect his faith in the idea that competition is not the point of his art or of the human enterprise in general. He represents this idea in his poem as a visionary truth which I try, in my way, to share.

✺

AFTER ISAAC LEARNED checkers, he pestered me for a long time to teach him chess. By then, he had started to think of math as a kind of game, and he was good at it. He kept asking to be given math problems in the car. I did simplified variations on problems from books. Once, when I was tired of this, I decided to give him a problem that would keep him stumped, and quiet, for a good long time. He was four.

The problem went: "At noon two trains leave stations in two cities a thousand miles apart. Each is traveling to the city the other is leaving. One is a regular train that averages sixty miles an hour, and the other is a high-speed train that averages a hundred and twenty miles an hour. What time do they meet and how far is each of them from where it started?"

This problem, to my mind, was evil. Isaac at four had never done a problem anything like this, and I gave just one clue, that they do not meet halfway, because they are going different speeds. He stayed quiet for several minutes. This was good, I thought, basking in my evil triumph. Dad needed a break.

Finally, he said, "I don't know."

I felt guilty, of course, for dampening his enthusiasm. It was OK. It was a tough problem. It was something he would learn about in junior high school.

He said, All right. But he knew, at five o'clock, the fast train had gone six hundred miles and the regular train had gone three hundred miles. That was nine hundred miles. So it had to be after five, but it was before six. At six they had gone too far. He said, that was as close as he could get. He was four. He had done this in his head, using the only tool he had for the job, addition. I talked him through the rest.

Soon after this, he became interested in a toy called the Magic Math Mixer. It was a handheld plastic disk with seven six-sided dice set in sockets, so that they could revolve freely to settle on any of their six sides. The central, black die was marked ten through sixty. The other dice, set around the perimeter of the disk, one black and five white, were numbered, each of them, with sides one through six. After you had spun the dice by sliding them over your palm to get a new configuration of numbers, you added the sum of the two black dice, the tens and ones. Then, the object of the game was to produce the value of that sum by using all the numbers on the five white dice, one time each, in a series of mathematical operations.

As soon as he started, Isaac loved this toy. He knew how to add and subtract, and he liked to use the toy to race against time. He quickly discovered, however, that any number over thirty was out of reach with addition. I taught him to use multiplication to get larger numbers. Division was easy after that. He learned to use his discovery that two and three were factors of six, and factors in general became important in his tactics. Once he got used to multiplication and division, after a few weeks, I told him he could also use the numbers as exponents, to get squares and cubes and so on. He learned the powers of two, up to the sixth power. He learned three and four to the third, and all the squares, including the squares of seven and eight, because these numbers sometimes came in handy. This process of learning took about two months.

The Magic Math Mixer has turned up just now, in a drawer where it has been sitting for many years. I spin the numbers, and get 50 and 6 on the two black dice. The goal is to reach 56. The white dice, clockwise from the black, are 5, 5, 2, 6, 2. Anyone familiar with multiplication notices at once that 5 and 2 make seven, 6 and 2 make eight, and eight times seven is 56. But these possibilities are a siren call, because they leave the second 5 unused. To compete in this game, you have to reject a cul-de-sac, like this one, instantaneously. So you try another way: 6 plus 5 is eleven, and eleven times 5 is fifty-five, plus 2-divided-by-2 is 56. Voilà! You can also get there using 5-plus-5 times 6, 6^2 or 2^6. Once you learn the game, this in an easy combo, lots of ways.

Isaac played with this toy so much he wore off the numbers, and he got another, the one still in the drawer. By the time he started preschool, he had mastered these operations thoroughly enough to race against me for answers and sometimes win. I did not like to let Isaac win in mental games, though it would have been too boring not to let him win in physical contests.

The Magic Math Mixer spins again. It turns up 40 and 3 on the black dice. This is a reminder. Isaac learned prime numbers at that age as well, because the concept helped speed the calculations in the game. The white dice on this roll are 1, 5, 6, 1, and 5. I am out of practice. Isaac at four would have beaten me this time. I see that 1 plus 1 is two, to the 5th is thirty-two, plus 6 is thirty-eight. The only number left is 5. Add that to thirty-eight, and you have 43. That's a good one. I like this game.

Isaac's calculations were not just memorization. He understood the principles, although his preschool teacher, who knew a good deal about childhood development, explained to me very gently that this kind of abstraction was not possible at four. She may have been trying to escape her embarrassment that such a small child was more skillful with numbers than she was. He had brought his toy to show to her. He liked her, and I did too, but we decided that she was not a good person for that kind of game.

After he began to develop his capacity for abstract thought, it was fascinating to see that he remembered less in the wide spectrum of incidental detail. He still remembered a great deal, but his eidetic memory, which had been uncanny, especially in a toddler, faded. He no longer knew the routes we took or the decor of all the places we visited. He never mentioned taking any account of this change. But he also forgot the names of the flowers he had learned, when they ceased to interest him. His memory for narrative, for many kinds of data, and for patterns of logical analysis, meanwhile, sharpened, as did his skills with words and numbers, skills that have stood him in good stead at the poker tables, where the player who can remember the most minute detail of other players' actions has an enormous advantage.

From our experience with math problems, I should have known better when I gave him a quick rundown of how the pawns and pieces move in chess. Skeptical about a four-year-old's ability to play, I spent less than a minute explaining. I was giving the complete information, but I was giving it at a faster clip than I thought possible to follow. I was trying to let him see that this particular game really was too complicated for him to enjoy just yet. He did not respond to the implicit point, however, because he learned the rules of chess in that one minute. He just said, "OK, let's play."

When we played, it took a few times for him to get the hang of moving the knights. A knight in the middle of the board can move to eight different squares, each of these, theoretically, by two routes. To plan a sequence of moves with a knight, a player needs to anticipate the sets of squares accessible in a series of positions. Isaac seemed to be learning these sequences after a few games. Since we both liked competition, once he had the overall feel of the board and was beginning to think in sequences of moves, I played him with a limited number of pawns and pieces, still trying to win. When he won three games in a row, with a particular handicap, I would add a piece or a pawn. We kept this up until he was beating me with the full set. By then he could play a game of chess in his head without the board.

At five, he won the first tournament he entered. Francie and I discussed his gift and agreed not to suggest lessons with a master. He enjoyed baseball, soccer, swimming, and other sports and games. We thought that to pursue a serious study of chess might narrow his interests and his social world. Besides, he was beating me already. There was only so much that a man could take.

THE DEVIL'S TRIANGLE

where
LOSS and THREATS of LOSS
AFFIRM
the *Value* of the *World*
we CHOOSE

B ECAUSE THE DEVIL'S Triangle does not exist, it would not seem to matter to the mind of reason that Isaac's winnings were in the Devil's Triangle, or that my wife and children had gone there without me. Things tend to disappear no matter where they are. Things everywhere go wrong.

In 1810, a body washed up on the shore of a small island in the Bahamas. The drowned woman was still holding in her arms a baby who was the sole survivor of the shipwreck. Precisely how the corpse could carry the still-breathing infant to the shore, my sources do not say. I picture the mother supine, draped over a piece of flotsam with her face submerged in clear blue water.

Almost fifty years later, one of the workers building a lighthouse on that island encountered the figure of a young woman searching that same shore at nightfall, crying, "My baby! My baby!" When the worker went to help her, he could see the full moon shining through her while it rose. At every full moon, people say, for over a hundred years, she wandered there and cried and searched in the moonlight, wailing.

I do not ask my reader to believe in the supernatural power of the moon. But in August 1969, not long after the first man set foot on the moon, the two keepers of the Gray Lady's lighthouse disappeared. This is an irrefutable fact. The island with its tower five and twenty fathoms high and ruined buildings at its foot, abandoned now by every living soul, is not a fiction but a real place called, I swear, Great Isaac Cay, near the western apex of the Devil's Triangle, just north of Bimini not far from where Isaac won his first big cash.

An apparition, people say, may announce a disappearance, and what disappears may come back as an apparition. The idea of the Devil's Triangle is itself a kind of apparition. Journalists, then psychics, and then science-fiction writers took three arbitrary points, Bermuda, San Juan, and Miami, and they called the lines connecting them the Devil's Triangle. They collected and invented facts to make this arbitrary figure interesting. As boys we read and talked about the missing airplanes and their pilots, the abandoned ships, their crews mysteriously gone without a trace, cryptic radio transmissions, fancy lights, winds, waterspouts, freak waves, discontinuities in time, and doors in space.

In 2007, Isaac, while he celebrated, was preoccupied with the sudden appearance of a particular sum of money, $861,000, and not at all with the mystery of disappearance in general. Francie had never thought about the Devil's Triangle, and neither had our daughter Miriam at thirteen, walking off alone into the dimly lit casino just after the tournament ended, with a vague idea of where the bathroom was and no sense of misgiving. At first when Miriam did not come back, Francie felt a little disconcerted. But she knew her fears were overblown. After a few more minutes passed, she had to wonder out loud, Where *was* Miriam? She did not ask Isaac, because she did not want to interrupt his celebration. But when he caught the tone of her remark to Lillie, he said, "Don't worry, Mom. I'll find her."

Francie told him no, to stay here, it was fine, but he just waved her off. Then, Isaac disappeared. While Francie waited she began to think that the security officers needed to organize a full-scale search. They needed to stop what might be happening to Miriam right now. When Isaac reappeared alone, he went with his mother and Lillie to the counter to inform the authorities, who asked for a description of the missing girl. Francie put her hand on Lillie's head. "She looks like this, exactly." The attendant at the counter nodded.

Isaac walked back toward the ladies' room. The messages were spreading, phone to phone to phone. Guards were searching everywhere, they said, within a twenty-minute radius of where the missing girl had last been seen. This sounded like a thing to do, except that everybody knew it was impossible. In five minutes you could walk outside and enter a car in the parking lot. In ten minutes, you could drive the car across a bridge and be in Nassau. After twenty minutes, you could be in someone's private plane in air, or in a boat at sea.

Isaac suddenly appeared again, unhurried. Was he *strolling*? He was joking now, with Miriam, approaching where their mother stood, and Francie, suddenly, was laughing too. It seemed that Miriam had merely zigged instead of zagged outside the ladies' room. She had wandered off between the rows of slot machines. When Isaac found her, she had found security already. She was not upset, so much as she felt silly to have lost her way.

Inside the Devil's Triangle, such silliness may disappear together with the person feeling it forever into an abyss. This time, what had happened was inconsequential. It was a fleeting dislocation, at its worst a flurry in a mother's mind. Or maybe, at its worst, it might have been the portent of a loss to come, a loss as sudden and as great as Isaac's winnings earlier that night.

In any case, to pay attention on a walk through any large casino is to learn that losing one's way is the rule. It's nothing to embarrass anyone. Casinos are designed as twilight labyrinths, where wanderers, who pause in their confusion, gamble more, and lose, before returning to reality . . . if real is what we want to call the part of the Atlantis where the visitors, whose savings pay for their escape out of the daily world, have come to wander. In that virtual realm, they walk together underwater, holding hands, inside a tunnel clear as glass. They look up at a manta ray much heavier than what any man could lift, yet weightless, flying in the perfectly transparent saline, tons of it straight overhead in the lagoon.

❋

I SPOKE TO Isaac on his cell just after he found Miriam, and I congratulated him on his big cash. It seemed likely that not having won first place, after coming so close, might interfere with his delight at winning what he did. But I was careful not to say this.

I said, "Way to go," and asked him how he felt.

He knew my disposition well enough to catch the drift of what I had not said, and answered, "How do you think I feel, Dad? I just won *eight hundred and sixty thousand* dollars. I feel good."

I had to laugh. "I guess you do. That's great."

❋

THE DEVIL'S TRIANGLE exists because things disappear. The universe itself, as far as we can tell, will disappear. If everything that matters disappears, and Isaac's winnings mattered, I was thinking, what a shame that is. I cannot seem to help the way I think.

Later that same year, Miriam gave up gymnastics, the activity that mattered most to her, and she grieved the loss. When Zoe was that age, she gave up ballet. Zoe's childhood self, the dancing Zoe, disappeared, and adolescent Zoe in her grieving disengaged from school. She persuaded her parents, after a few years, that the only way she would do better, the only way that she would stop cutting classes and start keeping up with things, the only way she would commit herself to making her life work, was to go to a school for actors, at the Interlochen Arts Academy in Michigan. She had been studying at Interlochen summer programs since second grade, and she loved the place. Her parents wanted her to stay at home in Chicago, but they finally agreed, her sophomore year, to let her go.

She discovered in her first semester there that one of the seniors, a boy she barely knew, had been smitten with her every year at summer camp since she was eight, and he was ten. This long-held secret devotion, in an older man, was irresistible. He was studying photography, and he left interestingly shaped bell peppers in her mailbox, suggesting a comparison between her and the peppers Edward Weston in his famous still-life photographs had revealed as something deeply sensuous, like nudes. Soon, her friend was photographing her, and they were in love.

Not long after he graduated in the spring, they found themselves at the top of the Ferris wheel one night, with fireworks going in the distance, and he asked her to marry him. She said she would. She thought that they would be great kindred souls in art, like Stieglitz and O'Keeffe. But on the telephone, between her dorm at Interlochen that next year and his at college, he sounded more and more distant, sometimes jealous, sometimes angry for no reason. He started telling her stories about implausible accidents and adventures, and she was unsure how to respond. He fell from the top of an enormous tree. He was trapped in a mountain crevasse. He would soon be traveling to Japan, because a famous architect invited him to photograph important buildings.

After some months of this, he broke up with Zoe on the phone, and when she pleaded with him, he came to visit her at boarding school. Suddenly, he wanted to be close, closer than ever. He wept with disappointment that she found these swings erratic, and he broke off their engagement again. After a few more months, she gave up.

He told her he was starting a job with the CIA. They wanted him to work with scientists, he said, to prove that time does not exist. Soon after that, during her senior year, he drove all day and all night non-stop to visit her at school. Uninvited and unwelcome, he appeared, holding out to her a single yellow rose, with which she hit him, before she threw it to the ground and ran away. He disappeared after placing the rose with the stem thrust into the ground where she had thrown it, as if it might take root and grow. It did not. It disappeared.

The following year, he emailed Zoe at Brown to tell her he was better now, on medication, and he had a son. His wife had left him.

＊

THAT ALL OF Isaac's winnings from the Devil's Triangle would disappear in a single instant might seem improbable even to the sad-sack disposition, except for the recent passage of the Unlawful Internet Gambling Enforcement Act.

The previous September, when Senator Bill Frist, Republican Majority Leader, had seen that a bill against internet gambling could not pass on its merits, he tricked the majority of his colleagues in both houses of Congress by removing the most substantial language and attaching the vague remnant to an unrelated bill which it would have been political suicide for anyone during the War on Terror to oppose, namely the SAFE Port Act. The bill resulting from this coup served in the short term as a talking point in the American Values Agenda for the Republican campaigns in the fall of 2006. In actual practice, the agenda involved circumventing the legislative process and introducing a bill at the last minute, so that no one on the Senate-House Conference Committee had seen the final language, and almost none of the Senate had time to review it, when it came up for a vote.

When poker players abide by the transparent logic of the game, they represent the value of honesty better than most politicians—better, in particular, than Senator Frist, whose management of campaign funds led to a conviction for violating campaign finance law. Whether or not Frist and other stock traders have been criminally dishonest, I believe that the stock market, like other forms of gambling, should be legal and that regulations on all financial speculation should be well conceived and properly enforced.

By January 2007, Isaac had been thinking about the so-called Unlawful Internet Gambling Enforcement Act for some months. Now, suddenly, in his PokerStars account, he had a sum of money large enough to make the issue urgent. Although his thinking about this situation was methodical, it did not cross his mind that moving his winnings to keep them safe from the quixotic enforcement of a spurious law would be the very choice that exposed him to the risk of losing them.

✳

THREE SUMMERS EARLIER, Isaac had been carrying boxes for $8 an hour, which was good exercise for a seventeen-year-old and not bad money, either, especially for someone more familiar with volunteer work. But the summer after his freshman year in college, he told us that instead of working another job like that, he wanted to play poker online. He enjoyed playing, after all, more than he enjoyed wage labor, and he felt that he could make more money at poker than he could at any job. Since Isaac's calculations tend to be accurate, his mother and I thought a summer of poker at home might be worth a try.

He played a few hours every day on his computer. I saw him at eighteen gambling every day for more money than I could imagine risking, and I thought that I needed to tell him what I knew from friends about the usual pattern of a serious card player's life. He wins. He plays for more. He wins more. When he plays for much more still, he plays against much stronger players, not all of them honest, and he plays at stakes so high that losing two or three big hands can be disastrous. When he loses and he needs to catch up on the loss, he loses more. By the time the pattern has played out, the wreck, the loss of everything, appears in retrospect so easily predictable that the whole scenario might have been printed up as a chart and handed to him when he bought his first handful of chips.

Isaac understood. He believed me, that what I had described was a common pattern. He said he had been discussing these issues in a forum on the internet. He was using the most reliable model he could devise to gauge his stakes relative to his bankroll, allowing for variance. What I had been telling him with the wisdom of age, he let me know with youthful tact which I found generous, he understood more thoroughly than I or my informants did. He said that he would have to ignore his bankroll management model with a vengeance, ever to let what I was describing happen to him. Since it was not in his character to be impulsive and oblivious, this would not happen.

Mathematically speaking, it could not happen, unless, of course, I was thinking, it did happen.

That summer, he made $40,000 in three months. This was many times his hourly wage of the summer before. It was also more than I was making then as a full professor.

When I was working as a file clerk at his age, I made enough to rent one room in a slum. There I read *Crime and Punishment*, a masterpiece about a poor, depraved intellectual, written after the author had bankrupted himself at the gaming tables. It was a novel perfectly tailored to my life and frame of mind. Although warm, dry, well fed, and in good health, I was down in the mouth. My happiness, I thought, required the company of a loving girl and time to read and write. Since then I have lived most of my life with both of these conditions met. My extraordinary luck in the long term has made it ridiculous for me to envy Isaac his returns at the poker table.

Speaking of luck, in 2005 Isaac and Zoe decided, as good friends, to spend Valentine's Day together, just the two of them. It was Isaac's sophomore year. By the beginning of summer, they were spending time together as often as they could, although Zoe stayed in Boston, where she had an apartment, and only visited in Providence to see Isaac.

That summer Isaac was assisting in the design of a computer program, a bot, which played a game involving the operation of a virtual factory in a virtual marketplace. The bot from Isaac's group competed with bots from other designers around the world in a competition sponsored by the Swedish Institute. Isaac's team did not do well that year, but the following year his faculty sponsor and the graduate student who had supervised his work designed another bot, which won an international competition.

Isaac explained his relationship with his supervisor by telling me about one of their conversations over lunch. First they sat for some time in silence eating their falafel sandwiches. Victor, the Russian grad student, then gave Isaac a searching look and asked him point-blank, "What do you think about the Cold War?" General Secretary Gorbachev and President Bush had announced the end of the Cold War at their conference in Malta about fifteen years earlier, when Isaac was five and Victor was eight.

Isaac said, "I don't think it worked out all that well, for anyone."

Victor nodded, and thought for a moment. "I agree."

Having settled this, they gave their full attention again in silence to the falafel.

When Isaac designed yet another gaming bot, as a final project for the artificial intelligence course he took with forty other computer science students, his bot won the class competition at the end of the semester. The professor gave him a B despite his final project's having outperformed the rest, because Isaac did not use the programming strategies he had studied in the course.

Isaac said that he understood all of those programs very well. Because he could see their limited potential in this competition, he chose other programs more effective than the ones his classmates had. This success, he said, demonstrated that he had mastered the material. If the professor wanted to test the application of particular programs, he should have designed a contest in which those programs would be more effective. The professor disagreed. I understand. Nothing is more obnoxious than an undergraduate who is pointing out an obvious defi-ciency in the organization of one's course. What made this worse was that Isaac was amused. It tickled Isaac that his professor, an intelligent and accomplished man adept in computer science, did not anticipate the kind of thinking that would win the game.

One last story Isaac tells about his experience in computer science involves two pages of elaborate code that he was about to hand in to one of his classes. The code was perfect, he told me, the product of some hours' work. Just as he approached the science library, a few minutes before the deadline, the paper slipped out of his hand in a gust of wind. It circled about fifteen feet over the stairs outside. When it caught in a tree, Isaac stood downwind. He could see that the staple was working loose and the two pages were about to fly. After several minutes, they swept past him overhead and swerved back into the leeward side of the building, which is the tallest on campus. From there they rose straight up along the wall of the library to the very top, fifteen stories, floating and swaying, until above the building they were swept away toward sea. Isaac told me he watched the pages disappearing into the distance at a great height, and he shook his head. By the time he was telling me this and shaking his head, a degree in computer science was for him a vanishingly small probability.

I asked him if he had told his teacher when this happened, and he let out a high-pitched laugh. "Who would believe that?"

Sometimes when Isaac was in the computer lab designing bots, Zoe played poker on his desktop computer back at the apartment. Isaac bought her a software program called Poker Academy, which included a poker bot designed by programmers at the University of Alberta. When she found that she could beat the bot in their program, she tried playing people online for funny money. When she saw that she was winning that game too, she tried micro-stakes. But she found that playing for actual money made the game frustrating instead of fun.

Meanwhile, Isaac played against the pros, and he kept winning. The more he won, the higher the stakes could be. At nineteen he was playing limit hold 'em at the highest possible stakes online. One big pot could be $1,000, or more, sometimes much more. He usually played six tables at once online, more than a hundred pots an hour. One night that summer, he dropped $20,000 in a series of unlucky hands. This was by far his biggest loss till then, and it happened faster than he could believe. It seemed, because it did not fit his winning paradigm, unreal. He felt shell-shocked, he told me some years later.

That night he did not talk to me. After losing, he sat down with a good friend, and they smoked. He never smoked or drank before he played, but afterward, he used weed, beer, and whiskey to unwind.

※

MY BROTHER RICHARD tells an interesting story about weed and loss. When he came home in 1969 from his tour of duty as a signal officer in Thailand, he was twenty-four. Because, according to sources in Thailand, the Army was studiously inattentive to what commissioned officers brought home, Richard packed a duffel bag with two large plastic bags of marijuana. He was alarmed, when he arrived at Yokota Air Force Base in Yokahama, Japan, to hear the name Lieutenant Richard Haxton called on the loudspeakers, asking that he report to a superior officer.

With his bowels twisted by fear into a noxious and gut-wracking uproar, he reported to the colonel's office and identified himself as Lieutenant Haxton. The colonel asked for his ID. Richard now felt sure that he was looking forward to some years in prison. He had been thinking that only one in ten bags was inspected. A nine-out-of-ten chance, prospectively, had looked golden. Any self-respecting gambler bets big with these odds. Now, in retrospect, the odds looked crazy. No sane person would take such a risk. He was not, after all, planning to deal weed in the States. He was just indulging himself by bringing home the stuff he liked to smoke with his friends. But a whole duffel bag full of weed, even though it cost him less than $100 in Thailand, made anything but dealing sound implausible.

The colonel, having inspected the ID, said that Richard's orders were to be the courier for a top-secret document to be delivered to a certain security officer in California. Something about this sounded wrong. Richard imagined a letter which read, "Send this man to Leavenworth; he's a dope smuggler." But there was nothing for him to say, except yes sir, and he got in line for his flight.

An army dentist, standing in front of Richard and boarding the flight from Yokota to Travis Air Force Base in California, carried in a paper shopping bag a sacred white gibbon, a beautiful long-armed, long-haired ape which it was illegal to export from Thailand and illegal to import into the United States. The dentist had tranquilized his gibbon and carried it with long limbs folded, as a package, sleeping, onto the plane. He had listed "gibbon" among his items to declare, and he expected the customs officer simply to check this off the list, which is, in fact, what happened. Over the Pacific, when the tranquilizers wore off, the white ape swung on the luggage racks up and down the length of the plane. Richard told me that he found this eerily peaceful, like a kind of ghost ballet. But his bowels did not return to normal. When the plane approached the coast of California, the dentist tranquilized his gibbon again to pass through customs.

At Travis Air Force Base, Richard was met immediately by two MPs, one of whom insisted on carrying his duffel bag. The MPs marched him around the customs checkpoint and brought him directly to a second colonel, a security officer, who, he had been told, was supposed to receive the top-secret document. Richard now inspected this second colonel's ID, as he had been instructed to do, delivered the document, signed various papers, and went from there, Ganesh and Hermes long be praised, to the Oakland Army Base. He processed out of his three years' enlistment, and from the San Francisco airport, as a civilian with contraband safely in his keeping, he took a commercial flight back home to Mississippi.

In his old bedroom at our parents' house, I inspected the stash. A scrap of paper in one of Richard's two huge weed bags said, GOOD SHIT. His ordinary weed, I soon found out, was stronger than the stuff I smoked in college, and the good shit was as strong as any marijuana on the planet at that time. This legendary strain now pales, however, in comparison with what geneticists have designed for Isaac and his friends to smoke.

If smoking were a game, the guiding principle of play would be connectedness and disconnection. We connect with an engagingly novel world in the intoxicated brain, and we disconnect from another world outside.

Property ownership uses similar logic. Possession is intoxicating, though absurd, as a way of defining my private connection to where I am. Meanwhile, it disconnects the place I own from others. Now, I may do as I please with what is mine.

The conduct of such games, the losses, and the winnings tend to appear very different from outside. Richard as a so-called volunteer could not quite lose himself in the military game. He saw himself from outside, but he had to play, and marijuana consoled him, especially when he was in Thailand. It helped him disconnect. Weed interested him less after the army, and music more.

After Isaac found her in the casino, Miriam lost gymnastics, which was a game she loved. Zoe lost dancing. Their lives changed. Each of these losses, and Zoe's boyfriend's loss of her and of his sanity and of his wife—each loss is absolute.

Isaac's loss of $800,000 might be considered trivial if we could establish that money is merely a game and that the arbitrariness and absurdity of money disconnect it from a sane estimation of value. But in this story dancing, gymnastics, and poker matter. Money matters as a way of keeping score. It matters how someone feels, when he sits at his computer absorbing the reality of a loss.

❋

FIRST, TO RETURN to the summer of 2005, Isaac lost more in one night online than many poker players lose in a lifetime: $20,000. I cannot imagine. Getting stoned and watching *Battlestar Galactica* under these circumstances, even with a good friend, I am told, is not a ticket to euphoria. Isaac kept trying to forget his loss, but it was too memorable. The loss was more than his winnings of the past several weeks, money enough to cover his living expenses for a year. He and his friend, who was laid up at the time with a hurt back, made silly jokes, while the bad vibe lingered.

The next day, Isaac felt a little better, but he had doubts. He went back systematically over the game of the night before. As usual, he could remember every card in every important hand, and every player's bet at every point. He remembered all this even though he had been playing six or eight tables at a time for some hours. I find it difficult, as an experienced poker player who has logged hundreds of hours at computer games, to move and click the mouse quickly enough to keep up with four tables on the screen. When I do this, I have very little understanding of the finer points of the game, and I remember almost nothing but a blur. When I do this for play money, I can win only when the other players are more thoroughly incompetent than I am. Isaac, while playing against professional gamblers on ten or twelve tables at once, can form a distinct understanding of most of the important players' patterns of play and develop effective answering patterns while remembering relevant details.

But Isaac's brain was not the only recording device he used. The data from the previous night's game were also in his tracking program. Every serious poker player online uses tracking software to store and quantify the history of his play. Isaac saw clearly, in retrospect, that his play had been better, by purely objective measure, than his opponents'. The other players got lucky, many times in succession, and Isaac got crushed. This happens. Still, he could reasonably expect to win against comparable opponents over a statistically significant sample of hands, although this kind of setback would also happen from time to time.

His bankroll was not seriously depleted, but he let what had happened settle in his mind while he played at lower stakes to make up what he lost, and more. Toward the end of his junior year, the high-stakes limit games again did not go well. He stopped winning for more than a month. He tried adjustments, but nothing seemed to help. Maybe it was the run of cards.

In June, he took a trip to Vegas, where he staked his friends from Brown as players in events at the 2006 World Series of Poker. This was the year before his big cash at the PokerStars Caribbean Adventure. He was twenty, too young to play in the Series, but he hankered for big action. He wanted to make the scene, the biggest poker scene on earth. Isaac believed that his friends were sharper than the players he had been getting to know online and that these online players were likely to be among the strongest in the tournament field. None of his friends had studied poker as carefully as Isaac had, but they were old enough to play, and they were math nerds in the Ivy League like him. It seemed likely that they could pool their various skills and resources and win.

They made staking arrangements, and Isaac paid thousands in entry fees for games where he was not allowed to play. The whole crew stayed together for two weeks, with Isaac footing the lion's share of the bill, the five of them in one hotel room in the Luxor, a building which looks from a distance like an obsidian pyramid. They played long hours every day, lost steadily, and returned to their little box inside the black glass pyramid to sleep. This was not the kind of fun they were expecting.

The high point for Isaac was when Zoe flew out for two days to visit. In the blaze of mid-July, they explored the Strip and loved it, knowing they would be back in their own room after dark. But Zoe had to be home for rehearsals and an opening in Boston.

By the time the whole crew headed east, one of them was spiraling into a deep depression and others had begun to grumble and to smell. If there were such a thing, mathematically speaking, the last few months would have been a losing streak.

But streaks are an illusion. In August Isaac and Zoe found an apartment with friends not far from Harvard Square. They lived well, eating at local restaurants, hanging out, and hanging in. With school about to start, Zoe was not looking forward to the difference between this summer and her life as a visitor in Isaac's room at Brown. The brothers in Alpha Epsilon Pi, the Jewish fraternity, were his people, nerds and gamers, and Zoe liked them. But frat life was not designed for her, and she was more important to Isaac than AEPi.

It so happened, as he learned years later, Isaac had missed by only one vote becoming president of his fraternity. If a tittle or a jot had shifted in one voter's mind, Isaac might have served his term as president that year, and Zoe would probably have done another year of theater in Boston. Their whole lives, in this case, might have gone differently.

As it was, after he got word online about the trouble in Congress, Isaac called the registrar at Brown and asked the penalty for taking a year off on short notice. When he found there was no penalty, he told Zoe the good news. Then he took a walk to think things through, before he talked to his mother and me. Our most recent conversations about college had been awkward.

During the previous three years, he had taken most of the required courses for his computer science degree: programming practice and its theoretical foundations, discrete structures and probability, artificial intelligence, programming languages, statistical models in natural-language understanding, and so on. Isaac was working harder in college than most of the people he knew. He had published in his field. He was on the verge of receiving a diploma with substantial value as a credential for work and for graduate study.

But one afternoon during his previous spring break, when he was looking out the window of the bus on his way back into Amsterdam from the big tulip gardens, it came to him that he could stop doing tedious assignments. He could stop taking courses he found dull. When he got back to school, the only thing he needed to do in computer science, ever, was to finish one team project so as not to leave his teammate in the lurch.

After that, he persuaded Francie and me there was *no* value for him in a computer science degree. He had chosen on the basis of aptitude more than interest. Now, instead of lukewarm interest, he was feeling antipathy. He planned to change his concentration to the philosophy of science, though he had little interest in philosophy either.

A substantial contribution in philosophy, he could see, would require maximum exertion from extraordinary genius. Good grades in philosophy courses, on the other hand, required less than this by several orders of magnitude, much less, for example, than similar grades in computer science. A serene acceptance of this fact was the essence of Isaac's philosophical position.

Luckily for us, the monetary value of his degree need not be the point. After growing up in comfortable circumstances, as my parents put it, Francie and I, even during the years when we lived poor, worked steadily and paid the bills. We could afford the movies we wanted to see, and we liked cheap restaurants. We bought the least expensive black-and-white TV at the discount store. Our furniture was mostly junk from the street, hand-me-downs, and secondhand bargains. It took us twenty years of this and that before we made good money doing work we deemed worthwhile. By the time Isaac was focusing on poker, I was a full professor and Francie had a thriving psychiatric practice.

Now, we wanted Isaac to find fulfillment in his studies and in his working life. As a freshman, sophomore, and junior, he chose what seemed to him a practical course. He earned good grades. But nothing caught fire in his mind. Later, he postponed his class work as long as he could, and did it in as little time as strictly necessary for earning an A. He made a game, in other words, of disengaging from school as much as possible, without diminishing the value of his transcript.

Zoe had similar difficulty finding her way in college. She had decided, after much deliberation, to attend Brown rather than study drama at the Tisch School of the Arts. She took to heart a comment from her drama coach, that an actor needs to know as much about the world as possible. She wanted to learn, and she wanted to use what she learned in her art.

But she could not find other theater students serious about the work in the way she wanted to be. Few of them had done as much preparation as she had done in high school. Those most dedicated to theater were the most experimental, but they were not well read, and to her way of thinking, their approach was disrespectful toward the audience, toward whom a genuine artist needed to be attentive and generous.

Yet the very strength of this ideal was making it more difficult to commit herself to the program as she found it. The challenges in theater and in academic courses, especially mathematics, still looked to her, objectively, like what she wanted and needed.

But the spontaneous connections which she formed in high school, in her junior and her senior years, when she was working hard and everything seemed possible, had become unavailable. It was as if her mind reversed its magnetic polarity and the objects of her most concerted attention, which had been attracting her and which still appeared to her attractive, were now pushing her away.

She often found that when she reached the door of the building where one of her classes was meeting, her body did not carry her inside as she had expected, but wandered to another destination, which she had not been considering, maybe a coffee shop or a friend's room. She lost her initiative and her ability to concentrate. Her mood kept sinking.

Instead of choosing what she wanted and thinking and feeling her way into what she chose, she found that her thoughts and feelings were working against her, like bad weather. It was a return of the mind-set and the mood that had troubled her after she gave up ballet, but why it was returning she had no idea. By the time she and Isaac got together, she had given up on school and was doing theater in Boston, but she found that doing theater away from college was not solving the problem.

The way Zoe had loved dancing and theater, Isaac had always loved, more than anything, to play games. Computer science interested him as a puzzle, but it became a chore. Lately, he saw that it was possible to make good money at poker, which was not a chore. It was a variation on his childhood fantasy, to be hired by Nintendo as a game tester.

The problem was not that he had lost interest in computer science, but that he had little interest in school. Like most undergraduates I have known at various colleges, he did not discover an academic concentration that engaged his passionate attention. Luckily, he found poker.

To say that Francie and I felt sad for Isaac would be misleading. He had moved away. We wept to see him go. But we were glad that he was thriving in his new home. He had made good friends. Zoe was the love of his life, and we loved her as well. A career in poker sounded odd, but it might be better for him than teaching or research. After watching him set out into the world from our safe harbor, we could see from his sails that he was catching a trade wind at the horizon.

So, while he walked up and down the streets near Harvard Square, past coffee shops and restaurants and bookstores, he was planning the conversation we would have about his plans. Not only was he giving up computer science now, but he was taking a year off from college, at the last possible minute, to play poker full-time. This did not sound, necessarily, like an easy sell.

When I say that Isaac was planning our conversation, I think about his charts for how he means to play a particular opponent in a heads-up match. He studies his opponent's play. He plans an opening strategy that will put pressure on his opponent's weaknesses. He estimates how far to take this tack. He considers various adjustments in response to his opponent's typical patterns and various ways of handling his opponent's adjustments to him. His work in computer science has helped him organize these choices in ways that maximize his chances for a favorable outcome. He uses something like tree structures in business models of hierarchical process design.

Isaac did not think of Francie and me as his opponents in a game. If life is a kind of game, which it often is, a family tries to play as a team. Still, he was planning for our talk the way he planned to play a tricky match. Isaac is like me in this, or like anybody else who analyzes what matters and tries to act accordingly. When I need to arrive at an understanding with others who think differently about concerns we share, the way I talk is tantamount to gaming. I find it impossible to imagine the absence of this resemblance. My formal training in rhetoric is different from Isaac's training in mathematical logic, but the results do tend to overlap. When effective planning and skillful improvisation help us to avoid pitfalls in our personal interactions and help to bring about a favorable outcome, skill in this game is a form of loving-kindness.

Isaac, in the game of talking up his project for the year off, had an inordinate advantage. He would be making his first moves before Francie and I even knew what game was under way. We were assuming that he would be going back to school in less than a month. When we heard his voice, we would both be happy just to talk with him. We would not be on our guard. He thought this through and sat with his cell phone on a bench in a little park.

When he had us both on the phone, he was direct. He trusted us to understand. He laid out a persuasive case in as few words as possible: "The law is changing. Internet poker may get shut down by the Department of Justice. I think, if I take a year off from school, and play full time, I can make good money. By the time I graduate it might be too late. I might have missed my chance."

I said, "How much do you think you can win in a year?"

Without pausing, he said, firmly, "A million dollars."

"Wow," I said. "That sounds good."

"Yeah. That sounds great!" Francie said. "A *million* dollars?"

This turned out for Isaac, and for Francie and me, not to be a very difficult game. We all believed that he could do precisely what he said.

❊

ISAAC WON HIS million dollars in the next few months. Now he worried that most of it might disappear. The Unlawful Internet Gambling Enforcement Act was already on the books.

During the last night of the slenderest possible crescent moon, before he went to sleep on Sunday, January 14, 2007, Isaac, to be safe, transferred $800,000 from his PokerStars account into his account at Neteller, one of the largest financial transaction services on the internet, a firm which often held hundreds of millions of dollars from corporations and from individuals. Isaac was planning to move the money again the following day from Neteller into a brick-and-mortar bank. This kind of two-step transaction was necessary because it was against the law for banks to deal directly with casinos. Antigambling laws had made Neteller gargantuan profits, by making the company necessary for a service that would have been superfluous except for laws that were themselves superfluous.

When he woke up on Monday, the crescent moon was gone, and Isaac found out from his poker forum that the founders of Neteller, two Canadian citizens living in other countries, had been taken into custody while visiting the United States. Stephen Lawrence, who lived in a luxury high-rise on Paradise Island, had been arrested in the U.S. Virgin Islands, and John Lefebvre on a visit to Malibu, California. They both stood accused, not under the new law Isaac feared, but under the Wire Act from 1961. Prosecutors said that Lawrence and Lefebvre had used electrical wires to exchange information in a criminal conspiracy to facilitate illegal gambling in the United States. The technicalities of this case are highly debatable.

Isaac's prize money, on the other hand, was definitively *not*, by any stretch of the imagination, the proceeds of illegal gambling in the United States or anywhere else. The tournament was completely legal under Bahamian law, as was Isaac's participation in it and the transfer of his profits. Still, when he tried to move his winnings out of his Neteller account, he was able to process only one transaction with a $20,000 limit before Neteller was shut down for all American users. The rest of Isaac's money, over $800,000, was seized "as evidence" in the case against Lawrence and Lefebvre. Isaac's money, in fact, had nothing to do with evidence. He was merely collateral damage in the prosecution.

Isaac's timing in the effort to avoid losing his money happened to have made him the one private person in the world with the largest sum of cash seized in this action. He assumed, at first, that his money would be returned, as soon as the prosecutors understood that he had not broken the law. After a few weeks, when he failed to get a thoughtful response from anyone in power, he began to wonder. Each week, at that point, the interest on $800,000 in a certificate of deposit would have been $800. This fraction of the total sum, a thousandth, may not sound like much, but it was nearly equal to the average wage in the United States, and approximately three times as much as Isaac had been making at his most recent job.

A more serious problem than lost interest was the fact that the IRS seemed to require payment of income taxes on Isaac's winnings, whether the prize money was returned to him or not. In other words, his winning $861,000 began to look like a net loss of $300,000.

Fellow gamblers, many of whom lost thousands of dollars in the seizure of Neteller, took various positions on the likely outcome of this case. After a few months, each entailing for Isaac the loss of more than $3,500 in interest on the prize money seized, he looked down the barrel of his six-figure tax bill and considered selling the contents of his account at a reduced value. One poker player well connected among businessmen at the top of the gaming industry tried to persuade Isaac that the prospects for the money seized were bleak. This good person would be willing, however, to assume the risk, if Isaac came down further on his price. Isaac declined the offer, but the correct play in this situation was far from obvious.

※

INTELLIGENT PEOPLE, SOME of them renowned philosophers, have found it impossible to prove that free choice really does exist, though most of us seem to believe that it does. If choices follow in a chain of cause and effect from the combined influences of circumstance and character, from genetics, education, and so forth, *free* choice must break free somehow from this chain, and no one knows precisely how.

Some experts say that games offer a distillation of freedom by placing us at a remove from the usual causes. To be truly free, they say, a player must be able to choose without the constraints of profit and loss, because the profit motive returns us into the bondage of causality. It's easy to understand their point.

But when the money at stake in a game introduces the profit motive as a strain of cause and effect, it must be possible still, if free choice really does exist, for the mind to break free. The very idea of freedom is predicated upon this mental power. If this power does not exist in relation to money, the apparent distillation of freedom in a game without wagering must be a sham. In poker the *freedom* of a bettor to bet as he chooses despite apparent constraints is, in fact, the essence of effective play. The money at stake does not *prevent* this freedom. The money is the *occasion* for the freedom.

The paradox of constraint and freedom is perplexing in what seems the simplest circumstance, for example, when we see bear cubs tussle on the ground and say that they are playing. The value of their game appears to us to involve their sensation of fooling around, in other words, their sense of freedom from necessity. When we watch them, we do not believe that the concept of freedom from necessity exists for them in words, but most of us can feel a similarity between their free spirit in the act of play and ours.

Their play, like much of ours, also may be represented as a practical pursuit, in their case, as training for the hunt, for defense, and for contests to establish mating priority and territorial prerogatives. For this practical advantage to be working, they need not articulate their goals any more than they need to articulate the concept of fooling around. The free delight of play exists in each of their minds, I would argue, just as the animals and their necessities exist, whether or not somebody happens along to refer to any of these presences by name.

In the case of a player *fading hearts on the river*, as I understand the logic of this phrase, the paradox is more acute. The mind of the bettor, having freed itself from *cause and effect* in the act of betting deceptively, yearns now for the opposite freedom, to free itself from the *randomness* of the fall of the final card.

❀

AFTER THE POKERSTARS Caribbean Adventure, articles about Isaac appeared in newspapers. He was interviewed and visited by a reporter writing a feature story on Isaac's life. Now he was more famous among internet players for the amount of money the government had confiscated from him than he was for winning that money in the first place. Still, his success made him feel excited about doing the tournament circuit. In March 2007, he played the L.A. Poker Classic at the Commerce Casino. This trip gave him a chance to visit with my brother Richard, who no longer used the cards or the good shit. For some years, Richard had been teaching English as a second language in adult education programs offered by the public schools. Meanwhile, he pursued his art as a musician and a songwriter.

The day after the tournament, Zoe and Isaac planned to meet Richard at the Los Angeles County Museum of Art to see an exhibit of paintings by Magritte. Because Isaac, in the tradition of Albert Einstein and Barry Manilow, does not drive, Zoe drove their rental car. They considered themselves lucky to find a parking place on Wilshire just outside the museum.

They met Richard near the entrance, where he sat, in the perpetual L.A. sunlight under the palms. He was writing the lyrics to a new song, which he would soon make into an animated cartoon for his website at hawkstown.net. He is, like me, our father's son. To an observer that day at LACMA, Richard and Isaac would have appeared an interesting match, both medium height, trimly built, with shoulder-length wild hair, Isaac's dark and Richard's lighter brown now gone to gray. The similarities in their features, and differences in age and bearing, made them the kind of people I like to watch in a museum.

Several of Magritte's most famous paintings were on display: the painting of the pipe, which has the sentence written in large script on the canvas under it, *Ceci n'est pas une pipe* (This is not a pipe); the painting of an enormous green apple filling a room, floor to ceiling, wall to wall; and the one of a small locomotive, maybe two feet long, which is emerging in midair from the back wall of an empty fireplace.

Magritte's clear presentation of impossibility strikes the mind at first as a joke, then as a visual provocation, a challenge to cognition, and finally it settles into its lasting character as a mysterious proposition for the mind and eye.

Zoe, Richard, and Isaac all enjoyed this. They enjoyed each other's company too, partly because they are a bit inscrutable themselves, as people tend to be, which may be why so many of us love Magritte. When the three of them left the museum and began to discuss the logic of how to get from there to the Yemeni restaurant which Richard thought they all might like, they stopped on the sidewalk a little way from the curb, and Richard asked Isaac where they had parked.

Isaac blinked, looked around, and said, "Oh, right there," pointing to the empty curb where traffic was now streaming past. Magritte had been preparing them for this perception.

The convenient parking place had been available, of course, because the city would be towing all the cars parked at that curb a few minutes later. When they found out where the impound was, Richard drove them there to pay their fine and fetch the rental.

On the drive, Isaac told Richard that they would want to avoid looking like drug dealers when they got there. Isaac thought that this was funny. They did look like outlaws. It was funnier because, in the trunk of the car, in Zoe's gray Swiss Army bag, with a little red insignia on the flap, Isaac had left not a duffel bag full of Thai stick or his own stash of designer weed, but his winnings from the day before. Isaac never traveled with marijuana and large sums of money together, because marijuana, according to the law, would make the money subject to irrevocable seizure.

"How much?" Richard asked.

"Forty-five thousand dollars," Isaac said, and he let out his characteristic high-pitched whinny of a laugh. This kind of cash, which he had won in the tournament, was ridiculous to him, and it was bizarre that he seemed to be handling such sums now on a regular basis.

Richard, having long ago retired from the poker tables of his youth, was trying to read Isaac. Forty-five thousand dollars was more money than Richard, in retirement from his job as teacher, would be needing to live for the next few years. Isaac had left this in the trunk of a rental car. But how did Isaac, barely having left the house of his childhood, feel about so much money being left at risk? It seemed incomprehensible to Richard that Isaac looked unfazed. He looked amused and watchful, but, overall, a bit opaque.

Isaac, meanwhile, had been thinking precisely the opposite about himself, because he had been playing J. C. Tran, one of a number of first-rate Vietnamese players in the L.A. Classic. Tran, who came in second in the tournament and won more than a million dollars, was as skillful as anybody Isaac had ever observed when it came to reading his opponents. That year, Tran would cash in twenty-seven tournaments and win three. Only four players in the world won more prize money.

Isaac felt as though each flicker of his own face muscles, every movement of his hands when he handled the chips, each shifting of his posture, every breath, every modulation of his voice, for Tran, was a perfectly legible index of his thoughts and feelings. Tran outplayed him steadily, because Tran could read him cold in every hand.

Isaac had played well and finished ahead of nineteen out of twenty players among nearly eight hundred entrants. He had won more than four times the $10,000 entry fee. But the main thing he was bringing away from the L.A. Classic was not the money, if the money in the Swiss Army laptop bag in the trunk in impound still was his to bring away. The main thing was his sharper knowledge of the need to read other players more discerningly, while revealing less himself. Card players carry this way of thinking away from the table, whether they want to change their inner lives or not, just as actors may sound stagy in their time off and teachers get pedantic. Isaac was thinking that he should seem unremarkable to the officials at the impound lot. This was the way to play the hand. He was also thinking, if a poker player at his level feels upset to make an ill-considered move and place $45,000 at risk, or $800,000, for that matter, he may need to find another line of work.

SALT CITY

where
brokenhearted YOUTH
DEVOTES itself
to *Images*
of what might
BE

WHEN I WAS growing up in the Mississippi Delta, snow was something from another world. My kinsman in that world, I would have said, was the abominable snowman, a creature like me, on the margin of human existence. I read about him in a book that belonged to my father, *On the Track of Unknown Animals.*

Thirty years later Francie and I moved our family for my teaching job in Syracuse, where she felt that I had delivered us all to the margin of human existence. That year the total snowfall here was more than sixteen feet, a record, although other years have since come close. In parking lots the plows left heaps of snow two stories high. At the end of the driveway the pile from shoveling was over my head.

After I shoveled the sidewalk, when the girls were toddlers, they liked to get dressed up in their snowsuits, cinch the hoods, and let me toss them up so that they sank softly on their backs into the deep snow in the yard.

I told Isaac about my fascination with the abominable snowman, mainly because I knew that he would like the word *abominable,* a word attached to the creature, it would seem, by Eric Shipton during his expedition to the Himalayas in 1951, when he photographed a famous set of abominable tracks.

When Isaac started playing Magic: The Gathering almost every weekend in the tournaments at the Magic shop, he showed me Mountain Yeti, one of the red cards in the deck. It depicted an apelike person in profile, with a long upper lip and thick cinnamon-red hair all the way down his sloping forehead. Beyond the close-up profile of the face was another image of Yeti in the distance, as a dark orange blur, a walker on the verge disappearing into the snowstorm.

Yeti was also the nickname of another regular player in the tournaments, a big man in his thirties who worked the night shift in a nursing home. Sometimes he would come straight to the Magic shop after pulling a double shift, his hair disheveled around the edges of the Oakland Raiders baseball cap he wore with bill dead level, his gut inside his T-shirt hanging over his belted jeans.

The boys asked Yeti sometimes if it was true that he ate cat food while saving up to construct a better deck. When he was feeling sly, he used to say that he did, and add with a cryptic shrug that he had not eaten cat food in a long time.

He seemed to tolerate the teasing as a sign that his good standing in the Magic crowd included what might make him unfit elsewhere. This was the essence of the Magic players' pact, strangeness accepted, the power of Yeti disappearing into the snowstorm. If the opposition used white cards to attack, white being the color of absolute righteousness, not necessarily for the good, Mountain Yeti was a red card, a card imbued with fiery passion, which you could play to fend off the attack.

*

IN 2007 PROSECUTORS were paid to argue that Isaac's money from the Devil's Triangle had been disappeared into the federal coffer in the service of a just law. They assembled for their case the equivalent of a white deck, a deck of righteousness not necessarily for the good. Isaac had a financial interest in taking the opposite view. He was playing a red deck, a deck of passionate devotion to individual freedom.

Isaac consulted with lawyers who were quick to tell him that he needed their good counsel. He should retain their services at exorbitant hourly fees as soon as possible. They were playing a blue deck, a deck which celebrates the powers of deception. Not one of these professional paragons, so eager to help a young person in distress, could specify when asked exactly what this counsel would accomplish. None of them seemed to understand, or even care about, the different legal status of funds seized as proceeds in an illegal activity and funds seized as *evidence*, not deemed to have been part of any criminal transaction.

Legislators, courts, and prosecutors disagree about the definition of "illegal gambling," but for lawyers to bill Isaac for a nonexistent benefit is what people generally call a legal practice, as if it had been proven more ethical than an honest game of cards. Reason is nothing, our best mathematicians and philosophers tell us, if not the seat of paradox.

Meanwhile, Isaac had disconnected from school, and he was disappearing into the game of poker. He was working the connections and the disconnections, the way gamers do. To understand Isaac's pursuit of various games, it helps to consider two of the sources of his gaming disposition, and of mine: my mother and father.

❋

MY FATHER LOVED to read about animals in their native habitats, but he preferred to stay indoors. For fifty years, the east end of the couch in the living room, the spot for which his stereo was balanced, was his own native habitat, in a house he had designed himself.

He formed a symphony orchestra in his hometown and taught himself to play whichever instrument was needed at the time, viola, cello, bass, English horn, clarinet, oboe, and bassoon. The musicians practiced in our living room.

He composed at the piano. He directed musicals and plays, for which he conceived and constructed sets. He seldom traveled except for his work as manager of a clothing store, but when he went to shop for the season's clothing lines in New York City, he spent more time in museums, plays, musicals, and art exhibits than he did in the Garment District. He wrote fiction. He lived in books, music, and games, while he made his living playing dress-up.

At the end of his marriage, my father was carving and painting wooden dinosaurs and large mammals prehistoric and still living, pteranodon, mammoth, giant sloth, gorilla, springbok, triceratops, kudu, and others. The work of making more than a hundred of these figures occupied him for some years. He gave the sculptures to his grandchildren. The pieces were never toys. He seemed to think of them as something closer to reality than art. I cannot say precisely what, not totems, not exactly. A phrase keeps drifting into my head like a Zen koan: *as close as he could come.*

As a boy my father prided himself on an animal skill at walking the tightrope. This is not a figure of speech. The tightrope was pulled tight between two trees in his backyard. During the Depression, he would juggle while balancing on the rope. He also rode a unicycle, did tricks on the trapeze, and liked to practice flips and twists off the high diving board.

Miriam and Lillie have inherited my father's acrobatic skill and a knack for numbers, both gifts from his father, the quarterback who taught math, and from his mother, who danced scandalously barefoot on the stage of the Public Theater in Greenville, Mississippi.

For this, Ellise Blum was denounced from the pulpit of the Hebrew Union Temple. A common sequence in our DNA may also have disposed the great-grandson to be smitten, like his father's father's father (and like the protagonist in his father's first book), with a beautiful dancer.

※

WHEN MY MOTHER took up chess in early middle age, my father gave her a board of precious inlaid wood from China, with pieces delicately carved in ivory, elephants and battle towers, horses, horsemen, sage advisors, king, and queen. My mother's best friend, Libba, with whom she played, was his good friend as well, whom he had known from childhood, a gifted artist, especially in watercolors, funny and kind. She and my mother, who were, unlike him, estimable drinkers, had fallen in love. Their games of deception went beyond the poker table and the chess board.

Love is not a game, and this affair was one of the great loves in both women's lives. But my mother had to break things off with Libba, she told me later, when the drinking went too far. Decades later, when my teetotaling father fell in love with a younger man, she felt wounded and humiliated, and in jealousy and rage, she had to leave. His losing her appeared to me the great regret of his life. After she left, my father's affair ended, for the sake of the young man's wife and children, it was said, although that divorce as well soon followed.

Marriage is not a game, but there is competition. We compete for tokens of our standing with each other, for space in the marriage bed, for money, and for time. Affairs compete with marriage. Spouse competes with lover. My parents were not especially contentious, but the competition in their marriage played until the end, beyond the end.

A family is not a game, but it is a system of illusions shifting in the minds of everyone involved, with moves and countermoves, truth always open to question.

Neither my father nor my mother found anyone with whom to share their later lives.

When Isaac took up chess, my mother gave him her Chinese set.

※

WHEN HE WAS eight, Isaac asked me to buy him his first Magic deck, cards full of pagan lore and mythical imagery, with scores of exotic words, like *basilisk, wurm,* and *wraith.* The lost medievalist in me, last seen before Isaac was born, took one look and wakened from his sleep. I wanted to share my old enthusiasm with my son.

The designer of the Magic deck was not a medievalist. He was Professor Richard Garfield, a Ph.D. in combinatorial mathematics, who had played Dungeons & Dragons in his youth. In the game of Magic, he drew from the lore of enchantment and myth and organized the data with a computer programmer's devotion to convoluted systems.

The rule book recommended that the beginner read all forty pages first and then go back and follow the details more slowly, step by step. After skimming the book and starting again at the beginning, I got irritated with Dr. Richard Garfield, Ph.D., and I wondered why anyone would design a game with such elaborate, confusing rules.

Isaac ignored the rule book. He played with his friends by making up a game to fit the cards. When he started playing at the shop years later, with players who knew the intricacies, he told me the game was fun, once you got the hang of it. The challenge was to construct a deck that won against opposing decks, despite the random order of cards drawn. There were cards that provided resources, and other cards that performed actions using those resources. The general character of a card was consistent with its color. Besides white and red, there were green cards, associated with growing things, black cards, associated with illness and death, and blue, the color of intellect and trickery.

Isaac joined the regulars at the Magic shop after he broke up with his girlfriend in ninth grade. They had been a serious couple for a year, which is a long time at that age, and they had worn each other out, the way most teenage couples do. Isaac was relieved when they broke up, and he thought she was too. Her need to spend hours on the phone with him every night made him think that things would never be quite right.

In the Magic shop, the people facing off, on folding chairs at long tables, were mostly teenage boys. The youngest players were ten or eleven, and the oldest in their fifties. There might be one girl among the dozens of boys, but more often there was not one girl. There was never a woman. Many of the regulars, like Yeti, were social outsiders in obvious ways. One, who wore a parka all the time indoors, spoke in a loud monotone without affect. Others were unkempt, obese, too shy to speak, cranky, or impervious to social cues.

A few of the men were creeps who came to touch the boys. If the shopkeepers had to call one of them off, he never came back. Hostile remarks about being gay were common there, and most of the creeps seemed to decide on their own that this was not a place for them. If the culture of bigotry in the Magic shop suggested that the bigots were uneasy with their own sexuality, which I believe that it did, it also suggested a smoldering hatred, as repulsive and as dangerous as child molestation. Narrow-mindedness among those victimized by narrow-mindedness is glue in many social groups. Bohemians dislike preppies, hoi polloi dislike the country-clubbers, intellectuals dislike ignoramuses, and so on.

❋

MANY OF THE fiercest oppositions in the world involve the competition between faiths, and faith in skepticism, like any faith, can be fanatical.

While I am writing this, from time to time I pick a blueberry out of the small bowl on my desk. Some skeptics believe we cannot know for certain whether the blueberries exist. Many forms of willful stupidity come into fashion among otherwise intelligent people.

I believe that things exist. These blueberries which grew in local earth are small, tart, and resinous, the way I like them. I pop one into my mouth. When it bursts between my closing teeth, I note its firmness, sweetness, tartness, drenching juices, pulp, and skin.

I know I cannot trace the unity of these impressions to a single area in my brain, as I would like to do. They merge inexplicably into the seamlessness of my experience. Records of disjunct sensations, touch and taste and smell, after a split second perceived as an almost instantaneous memory, are *as close as I can come* to being in the actual moment of eating a blueberry. My eating of the blueberry is a celebration of the mystery of being in the world.

The sources of deep skepticism are clear, meanwhile, even to me. The so-called present, by the time I know it, is a memory. The world cannot be known except as an illusion. Thus, enlightenment in some schools of thought is the spontaneous and infinite delight in nothingness as the ground and essence of the illusion of being. This idea fuses faith and skepticism in a way I find sublime.

But I believe that things exist. Representations, to my mind, indicate those actual things. Isaac represents himself effectively by using cards. Winnings represent for him an authentic value in his play. To have his $800,000 snatched away is painful. The distinct absence to come of that money in his life is real. When he hopes to get that money back, to come *as close as he can come,* if coming close means failing to recover a thin dime, may be spontaneous. It may be infinite. But it is not the wellspring of delight.

❊

MY FIRST THOUGHT, when I saw the Magic players, was, they look like poets. A colleague from India had told me that in her language the expression "You look like a poet" means you have neglected your appearance. My grandmother used to say, "You look like something the cat dragged in." My colleague took great pains to clarify, because I would not stop pretending to take her insult as a compliment.

Those in the shop who presented themselves most artfully, in outlandish makeup with dyed hair, fantastic outfits, piercings, and tattoos, the people dressed as vampires, witches, and warlocks, were not

Magic players. They played Dungeons & Dragons. The Magic players thought that dressing up and acting out fantastic scenes, like those depicted in the Magic deck, was silly.

The sixth edition of Warhammer deserved respect for its serious emphasis on strategic combat, but most Magic players were not skilled in the meticulous art of painting model soldiers, creatures, and terrain. The beauty of the art was crucial to the player's prestige. It was amazing to see these war-gamers with elaborate daemons, warriors, ships, and castles assembled for play on a table big enough for an elaborate train set. Nobody seemed to play both Warhammer and Magic with equal passion. The differences between games were regarded less as questions of taste than as marks of the player's identity. Still, for me, the identity of the Magic player is mysterious.

In every Magic player's more-than-conscious mind is a fantastic realm, elaborated by four hundred professional artists who have painted images for twelve thousand different cards. At dawn the kraken's eye has washed up onto a desolate beach. On an island, in an ocean haunted by merfolk, masts from shipwrecks tilt among the palms. Beyond the swamp, across a desert, over the mountain crag past live volcanoes, in a forest where the golem lives, a shaman has the djinn to perform his will.

Virtual realities have been my calling. Even when readers find what I have imagined in language gratifying, however, the value of what I do has never been quite clear.

Billions of people, including me, have spent hours at a time in the virtual realm of television. I dislike moralistic objections to this. My great-great-great-great-grandfather must have objected to his daughters' pleasure in attending the ball, for similar reasons. I do not know why people need a world of dreams or waking dreams, but fantastic pleasures seem to be more deeply seated in our nature than the prohibitionists' denials.

Six million boys and men are players in the realm of Magic, making their way among their peers as wizards. You might think they would regard themselves as wizard-like in real life. They do not. Magic players practice sorcery no more than fans of TV shows about extraterrestrials prepare for the invasion. Many players who spend hours every week on the selection of cards for their constructed deck mispronounce the names of the mythological beings on the cards.

If a Magic player's inattention to mythology seems strange, it must seem equally strange when a poker player holding four cards to a Broadway straight does not care which of the figures in the French court may have been depicted on the face card that he lacks. Almost any child discovering the face cards must assume, as I did, that the meanings of these pictures matter in ways the grown-up players understand: the swords held by the jack of diamonds and by three kings, the one in hearts with blade upraised behind his head as if to strike a blow; the battle-axes of the king of diamonds and the jack of hearts; the different flowers held by different queens; the feather in the one jack's cap; the leaf in another's hand; the faces turning left or right, in profile or three-quarter view. All of this must matter to the game, to be preserved for centuries by hundreds of designers of new decks.

The symbolism of the ace, the smallest number and the strongest card, seems most mysteriously charged of all, a token of the One Prime Power, Alpha and Omega, for whom it is written that the last shall be first, and the first last.

But almost no one playing poker cares about these things. If I have four cards to a Broadway straight, I want to fill the straight. That's all. I want to win. Why I want to win, when I stop to think about it, is no less mysterious than the images on the cards.

※

COMPETITION IS NOT the only appeal in games any more than it is in writing. Because game scenarios interest me as representations of the world, I have been reading in a fifty-year-old book a psychoanalyst's description of the game of chess as an Oedipal scenario. Freudian thought has been under attack for more than a hundred years. I find the criticisms from neuroscientists, sociologists, historians, and feminists persuasive. Most serious readers, I suspect, consider Freudian thought an artifact, like Ptolemaic astronomy or alchemy. But the Freudian system is also mysterious to my mind and compelling, just as alchemy is.

In chess, the psychoanalyst observes, a king is a father figure. Each player wants to overcome an opposing Father to control the only viable Father on the board. The game appeals to a young man who wants to displace an opposing father. To disguise bloodthirstiness, the rule is that the opposing Father is to be trapped beyond escape, not killed. The most powerful piece in this contest, of course, is Mother, the queen. Touching any piece, except to move it, is taboo. An idle touch suggests that sensual pleasure is the point and that play, except when fully engaged, is merely masturbation.

Adolescent male preoccupations might seem to distract this author from the real complexities of chess. But the psychoanalyst in question, Reuben Fine, also happens to have been an international grandmaster.

At one point, his chess rating was arguably the highest in the world. His Freudian interpretation may be old hat. But his argument has a strangeness fascinating even for those outside the circle of faith. In logic, after all, to ask someone if she believes in psychoanalysis is like asking her if she believes in chess.

Psychoanalysis, like chess, rewards the player's faith in a system of illusions. In the game of psychoanalysis, deep-seated feelings of attachment and anger are reenacted by the analyst and with the analyst. This game is designed to supersede earlier reenactments in the game of neurosis. According to Freud, the neurotic husband may feel compelled to reenact with his wife, for example, a troubled relationship with his mother. He cannot solve the neurotic problem in his marriage, because neurosis is a misrepresentation which conflates the present and the past. This distracts him from the more fundamental challenge, which is in his memory of a psychic wound from childhood. In the play of analysis, the psyche is freed from neurotic misrepresentation, so that it can then prove equal to the past, which has kept defeating it in the compulsive repetitions required by the game of neurosis.

What interests me in these scenarios, or in any game, is what interests everyone. We want to understand what we are doing, especially when we define the games more broadly to include such virtual realities as money, government, religion, war, art, and love.

We want to understand how it works for a game to disconnect what people do from ordinary circumstance, so that the logic of an action is revealed by distillation, then turned back, and reconnected to the world. We say, it's only a game, and then, to make it interesting, we play for money. It's only money. Money makes the game a business. It's just business, nothing personal, and besides, that personal stuff, it's all a crazy dream. Neurologists who specialize in dreaming tell us, meanwhile, that, without dreaming, memory itself, the seat of all experience, is disabled and reason comes unhinged. Then again, logicians tell us, reason also is a game, in which the rules cannot be made complete or clear.

The brain keeps representing all of this, despite the contradictions, as reality, and this makes neurophysiology one of the most fascinating frontiers at our moment in the history of human understanding. I feel drawn in that direction when I try to say what happens in a game.

A friend of mine, a scholar of Freud and a chess player, keeps several games in progress in his mind, to be reviewed in turn before he falls asleep. He tells me that his brain repairs and tunes itself while he plays chess. When he studied with a grandmaster as a boy, in the years of his adolescent obsession, he says, he must have laid down in his brain neuronal patterns which only chess can fully put to use. Because of this, all intellectual activity for him derives from chess.

Chess has made itself a nest of networks in his brain. Although he has become a scholar of literature and religion, grounded in philosophy, adept in many languages, an expert translator, composer, and musician, still, in chess, as in no other precinct of his mental life, the neurophysiology of his well-being thrives, and he believes the game may counteract the neurophysiology of sadness.

❁

IN THE DOOMSDAY poem Isaac made up at the age of four, he seemed to be looking with his wits about him into the source of his night terrors. By the age of eight, night terrors were long past. What might have been their crux had crystallized into a panic-ridden fear of death. When this awareness came to him, I felt helpless to console him, though I tried, because the same fear has kept seizing me from time to time since I was that age. Why some people feel this oftener or more intensely than others, I have no idea.

When this state of mind comes over me I feel my thoughts accelerate toward nothingness as though I took the car too fast over the crest of a hill. I cannot catch my breath. My guts flip like so many fish drawn up inside a net. I find myself ridiculous, contemptible, and powerless.

I tried in my teens to be more philosophical. But after reading Plato's report of Socrates in prison, unafraid, before he drinks the hemlock, I felt no more accepting of mortality, only more ashamed of my fear.

The trick that Isaac used most often in his teens, when he wanted to dispel his fear, was to spring out of his bed with a loud groan and to rush from his bedroom, as if the problem of mortality might occupy a certain space.

It does. The space is here.

❁

ISAAC ANALYZES PATTERNS of play as methodically as anyone he knows, and he enjoys a steady sense of fascination with the game. To have this native disposition is great luck. Even better, when he has played well, he understands that bad results are often outside his control.

All through childhood, in baseball, soccer, chess, and Magic, he started game after game expecting to play well, and then, if he had not won, he shrugged off the result. I felt grateful that he suffered relatively little from disappointment, but I never guessed how much this disposition would sustain him in his work.

When the U.S. Department of Justice took Isaac's money, at first he accepted with equanimity that what the government had done was beyond his control. He knew that he had not broken the law, he trusted that his money was being held in a legal proceeding, and he expected reimbursement as soon as the evidence seized had been reviewed.

He said later that this faith in the law was his main reason for not telling Francie or me what had happened. He saw no point in worrying us. Two months after the seizure, we received his phone call from California.

He had just given an interview he thought that we would see online. He was famous now, he said, for being the person with the most money confiscated in the Neteller prosecution. He was sorry for not having told us, but it was just beginning to dawn on him not to expect his money until the case was settled, which could take some months. At that point he expected full reimbursement, if no serious complication had arisen. Meanwhile, he said, he would probably be required to pay the income tax on his winnings.

❧

FROM CHILDHOOD ALL through adolescence, Isaac could not for the life of him hold still. Most teachers in our conferences would mention his contortions in his chair. In many of his classes, more than once or twice a year he tipped onto the floor, sometimes crashing sideways, sometimes backward, forward, desk and all. His brain was happy to concern itself with topics utterly removed from time and space, but his whole body needed to be working here and now, whether he was doing calculus or playing chess.

Zoe, meanwhile, had been devoting herself as a child, with obsessive discipline, to the precise positioning of every part of her body. She moved on the floor with aplomb dictated by the verticality of her spine, head upheld, shoulders floating, hips aligned, so that the turnout flowed in its perfection as the feet, bleeding inside her shoes, danced lightly into their seven positions, and the arms seemed to lift of themselves into the grace and balance of each posture. Her body moved as though her limbs were a perfection of thought.

When Isaac, on the other hand, was playing a game of chess, he twisted both his arms and legs in contortions, twirling his hair around his finger, leaning forward, sideways, and back, and his opponents, if they did not know him, thought that this performance at the margin of the field was gamesmanship. It had to be a deliberate distraction for someone so intelligent to fall, flat out, onto the floor. A chess player usually keeps his body still, to move only on the board, because a game of chess, unlike a game of cards, *is* movement in space and time.

A card game is less spatial and more purely probabilistic. When I discussed this difference with Isaac, he reminded me that spatial reasoning is the area in intelligence testing where he has always done least well. Everything else for him has always been at the top of the charts. But his spatial reasoning is not. I do not know how to square this with his ability, before the age of three, to remember the routes we took to his friend's house and the park. His ways of thinking, and his habits of memory, changed after the age of three. Whether his spatial reasoning has suffered from disuse I do not know.

Still, in poker, his impression of the cards most probable in his opponent's hand is spatial. Before he does the math, a picture takes shape in his mind's eye, a three-dimensional grid of cards. The cards are arranged in numerical order across the grid, with cards already exposed on the board and those in his hand much more distinct. In lines perpendicular to this array he sees cards that are likely to be in his opponent's hand, and these appear to swarm in greater numbers as the opponent's play suggests that the probability of their appearance is greater. If his opponent probably has a queen in his hand a swarm of queens will appear in the imaginary grid. Isaac says this model is not strictly organized, but impressionistic, with impressions accurate enough to use as a basis for patterns in betting without conscious calculation, except in unusual cases.

❋

LESS THAN A billion years ago, an early paramecium detected an obstacle in its path, directly at its bow, and it responded to the information by using its cilia to reverse, reorient itself, and pass the obstacle, so that it happened to find itself in another spot richer in the algae that it ate.

When earlier organisms detected obstacles and could not respond, the information about the obstacle yielded no advantage in their survival. But to *use* the information helped the ciliated ones survive and procreate, to pass along the same advantage.

For hundreds of millions of years, evolution has kept favoring quirks of physiology that respond to the creatures' surroundings. These quirks must have been selected long before they entered anything like what we now call consciousness. Evolution has elaborated the ways of gathering information, always in tandem with more elaborate ways of responding, so that a greater probability of survival has followed from action taken with a more and more probabilistic orientation in time and space.

An early tree shrew, when it smelled a snake, chose either to freeze or to run away. It might slip into a burrow or climb higher. If it chose well, it survived to procreate, and its offspring inherited its knack for making similar choices. A tree-ape, later, must have seen fruit hanging on a small limb over a hungry cat, and its chances of survival improved when it appreciated the risk in retrieving the fruit.

Fifteen million years thereafter, when I was a boy, several chess masters spent hours analyzing the most favorable play in a particular game before they consulted Bobby Fischer, who saw within a few seconds the flaw in their plan. Fischer was to chess what the ciliated opportunist was to the evolution of the paramecium, or what the tree shrew was to primates. The game of chess has evolved on the strength of his play.

Fischer's usual way of thinking through the game rested on encyclopedic knowledge of every game of the great masters. Having thoroughly assimilated this knowledge, he played by feel. Without precisely articulating it, he could use more-than-conscious spatial thinking in the calculation of probabilities. He sensed the developing topography of the game, the soft spots and the tangles on the board, and he acted on these impressions much as an outfielder does, when he pivots and breaks into a run in the split second of seeing the ball leaving the barrel of the bat.

The calculus performed in billions of synapses in the outfielder's brain in that one instant is more intricate in its mathematics than the life work of Newton and Leibniz combined. There is no written system more reliable than the calculus for mapping a path across the outfield to the point where the ball may be caught. The mathematics of the event is unspeakably complex. Part of the athlete's gift is instantaneously precise calculation, in the Boolean matrices of the neuronal maze, an inherited skill at computation refined by millions of years of natural selection in various species making coordinated movements in relation to the surroundings.

❊

ON OLD-FASHIONED SCOREBOARDS for baseball and football, the labels for the teams are Home and Visitor. In technical descriptions of hands in poker, whether in books, in periodicals, or in the forums online, the standard labels for the players are Hero and Villain.

No one is expected to think that either is heroic or villainous, but people find that the transparent inaccuracy of the labels fits the mentality of the game, because the essence of poker is the deception which permeates every feature of play.

After Isaac had spent years in the game, he took a serious look at himself and saw that his mind was wrong. When anyone in idle conversation at the table asked him a question, his instinctive impulse was to answer truthfully. Deceptive answers involved hesitation. This reflexive honesty, he realized, must make him less deceptive during play.

He thought about this before he started the World Series one year, and he made a rule, to avoid giving Villain any preview of his attitude toward deception. During that Series, when he spent eight hours or more in the casino about five days a week for six weeks, he would lie as much as he could without appearing to lie. Whenever he spoke to anyone on any subject, except when he was required to do otherwise by the rules of the game, he lied. He lied steadily to strangers, acquaintances, and friends. He lied about his personal life; about his taste in food, music, and clothing; about his education, his athletic abilities, his family, his religion, his leisure pursuits, and his political convictions. When he thought that he could do so undetected, he lied about the weather.

I asked him if he found doing this worthwhile. He nodded, and smiled.

＊

AMONG THE BEST poker players in the world, Isaac tells me, almost everyone has formed a general understanding of the mathematical problems posed by the game. They know the probabilities in a wide array of circumstances. But there is a striking difference between those like Isaac, who subject their thinking to mathematical analysis, and those who make mathematically sound plays, like the outfielder, without consciously crunching the numbers.

Josh Waitzkin, the chess prodigy whose childhood was depicted in the movie *Searching for Bobby Fisher*, turned to the study of tai chi after his early disillusionment with chess. In tai chi, formal movements articulate a player's way of being in his space, one player's way contested by another's. Waitzkin, who was many times a scholastic champion in chess, was also twice world champion in tai chi. He reports that, in either game, he observes his opponent's way of representing himself and responds by bringing his opponent to a position where that way of being is a disadvantage. In tai chi the computations which are so painstakingly slow in chess take infinitesimal fractions of a second. After his match with Isaac in the Devil's Triangle, Ryan Daut also became a serious student of martial arts.

When we saw Waitzkin play a demonstration match in Syracuse, he was unhappy in the game of chess. Celebrity had turned his mind-set inside out. Instead of immersing himself in the game, he said later, he seemed, in the grip of fame, to be watching himself through others' eyes from elsewhere. In tai chi he recovered his inner way of being.

Isaac's interest in chess tournaments was also starting to wane around that time, for different reasons. A certain girl, trained by her expert father, never lost a match in any of the local tournaments. Anna Levina was one of the top players their age in the country, and her game then seemed to Isaac virtually flawless, far beyond his reach. Too pristine, he said back then, to interest him. To put this same idea another way, her game made his game irrelevant. He saw how far behind he was by then and chose to let it slide. Anna Levina went on to distinguish herself on the chess team at Duke and in later competition.

Isaac at twelve loved baseball and soccer too, but he lacked the speed and strength to play at the level of his strongest peers, and his interest in athletics faded.

An orthopedist had recommended that Isaac as an infant spend some months in a special harness designed to jam the ball of his hip into its socket so that it would grow the way it should. This sounded to his mother and to me like torture. The desired result, if it occurred, still might not compensate for the neurological or psychological effects of being hog-tied for some months. Now, no one notices that one of Isaac's legs is slightly shorter than the other. His health is excellent, beyond what anyone could ask, but his athletic ability has always been limited by his hip, and by flat feet and crooked knees.

He might have gravitated into chess because of this, if not for that one girl, who had, like Reuben Fine, the double luck of being both a Russian *and* a Jew. India, in the person of Viswanathan Anand, reasserted dominance in world chess from 2007 through 2012, and, in 2013, Norway took the title for the first time, when Magnus Carlsen defeated Anand and earned the highest point rating ever recorded. I should say, while proclaiming ethnic triumphs, that a Japanese American and an Armenian American have been the two dominant players of the national scholastic game in recent years. Mapping the ethnic history of the game is more pleasing because the board itself is a map.

※

AFTER ISAAC BROKE up with his girlfriend at fourteen, he took stock. Because he had skipped fifth grade, he was the youngest in his class, and he was younger-looking than his age, less than average height, with not a wisp of real beard in his peach fuzz. His voice had not yet changed. He had good friends, but even to his friends he was the little guy who sounded like a brainiac from Mars. They liked him, but he was not cool.

Inside the Magic shop the purpose of existence, all that mattered, was the game. With his good friend Alex, driving to a tournament in Montreal or Boston, flying to the regionals in Chicago, where Alex came in first and Isaac second, he shared an elation beyond personal concerns. It was a triumph of sublimation, subordinating the accidents

of personal life to the logic of a game, where sound thinking anticipated accidents in play.

Nothing seemed to be at stake, and Isaac, feeling that he had nothing to lose, gave his all. The choice to do so was clearheaded. It was
a choice to be uncool. But in the uncool world of Magic, this choice
was sublime. One of many sweet reversals in that choice would come
when Isaac applied to college. Near the top of his class, with top board
scores and top grades on Advanced Placement exams, he still lacked in
any one pursuit the superlative achievement which tends to be decisive
in an application to any of the most competitive schools. In his essay
for Brown, where the admissions office invited an unconventional
approach, he wrote about his passion for Magic. He believes his essay
probably decided his acceptance.

He spent the summer before college working a crummy job all day
and playing Magic at night. Some nights he played poker. For years
I had been telling him that poker was a good game. Now his Magic
friends, who had more credibility as gamers, told him he should check
it out. They found poker at the casino similar to Magic, with a funny
difference. None of the other players in the poker room, though they
were risking serious money, really tried to win.

With friends from school, the ones who thought Magic was a joke,
the good part came when they found out how the joke goes at the
poker table.

❄

AFTER HE GRADUATED high school, Isaac thought about the way
his friends had classified him as the ultimate nerd, and he decided not

to be that person anymore. When he got to college, he dropped Magic. He played poker. Partly because he was now average in height, he also found that college girls, unlike girls in his high school, were interested from time to time, when he was interested in them.

His mother and I, without a clue that poker would be anything more than entertainment, gave him a set of poker chips for his birthday. Early in his second semester Isaac played a game for much higher stakes. The other two players that night were fellow students in computer science. One of them, the one who pushed toward higher stakes, happened to be the son of a tycoon, the Donald Trump of Tokyo, someone said. The third player in the game was Scott Seiver, one of Isaac's friends who would be with him at Nobu in the Bahamas. The junior tycoon was a brilliant computer scientist and had a strong competitive drive in games, but he lacked the gaming chops which have since made Isaac and Scott world-famous in poker. For now, all three of them were just beginning to explore the game. On the dingy carpet in the common room of a dorm, they sprawled and played almost until dawn.

Isaac loved the exhilaration of winning hundreds of dollars. When the game ended, he had to cross the deserted, frozen campus alone. Winning in poker felt different from winning in Magic. A game for serious money placed him at another social margin, but this one, almost everybody thought, was cool.

With his fancy chip box under his arm, big winnings in his pocket, and his heartbeat in his ears as loud as a public address, he was thinking, if ever there was a time and a place for a mugging, this is it. He could not imagine that he would be carrying one hundred times this sum on a regular basis within three years, much less that the mugger, when more than a thousand times this sum was stolen from him, would be the Department of Justice. Still, he knew that something unusual was happening. He was frightened, and exhilarated. But he did not yet know that he was starting to take stock of his career.

PROVIDENCE

where
MEMORIES abscond,
DREAMS threaten,
and sheer LUCK
Prevails

S URPRISED TO FIND myself in the emergency room of all places, I asked Francie, "What happened?" Somewhere in the middle of the night I had hurt myself, she told me, and I came home confused and covered with blood.

Now they were stitching my head and bandaging my hands.

Three minutes later I was surprised, again, to find myself in the emergency room of all places, and I asked Francie, "What happened?"

Whether the injury had caused my brain condition, or a brain condition caused my injury, no one yet could say. For some hours I had been unable to remember much of the past or to keep track of what was happening at the moment.

I would like to describe how this felt, but I cannot remember.

❀

THOSE MOST PRACTICED in the art of memory two thousand years ago found that they could remember more by imagining each thing in a particular place, say, in a particular room of a familiar house, so that, when they walked in memory through the house, they found things where they had imagined them.

I remember pieces of music as ways of positioning my fingers to play. Without the instrument defining the space for my fingers, I forget details of the patterns of sound.

When I memorize words from a printed page, the typographical spacing helps. But after I have a poem by heart, I forget the space on the page, and I search in the vacancy of my mind for where to begin. A phrase floats up from nowhere, while the rest of the poem often remains hidden from consciousness. When the phrases form in my throat and in the muscles of my tongue and larynx, lips and jaw, they return into my mind.

What arrives is not just words. A long-dead poet's intimate imagining wells up in me, imbedded in the words, in Greek or Latin. Out of nowhere comes a voice. It speaks a language I have difficulty reading, yet it comes to life with overwhelming thought and feeling. In a poem by Zonas, a Greek father describes his son, a toddler too young for sandals, stumbling as one of the dead on the far shore of the River Styx, and the consciousness of grief and longing, memory carried in the act of speech, rides again like a surfer on the slope of a collapsing wave. This time I am the wave. I could not find this more mysterious than I do.

❊

IN THE CONSTRUCT of words, writer and reader come together apart from what words represent, apart from where the writing and the reading happen to take place.

Language defies distance. Between Isaac and me at the moment is the Atlantic Ocean and a great swath of the Mediterranean Sea. He has settled with Zoe in the island republic of Malta, near where Gorbachev and Bush conducted their summit when he was five, not far from huge stones that were constructed into buildings five thousand years ago, buildings made by people long forgotten by the time of the pyramids or Stonehenge. Yet here those people are, together with Isaac, in this sentence.

My mother has just died, and I have been dreaming about her night after night for several weeks. I wake up before dawn. I make strong coffee and come back to my desk to write. I want to write about her too. When I write from memory, I want somehow to disconnect from the present, and make past connections stronger.

Representation is a doubtful business, in games, in dreams, or memories or ruined constructions of gigantic stones. I hope it clarifies my interest in this problem to present a mental challenge about which no one can remember anything at all, even to misconstrue it: I look, and there I am in the mirror, with blood all down my face, and on my hands and clothes. I look at myself, and I try to remember how I got there.

※

I CANNOT REMEMBER walking home at midnight with Miriam's bloody kick scooter in my hands. When I laid it just inside the front door and went upstairs, I might have been preoccupied with trying to understand what had happened. Maybe I was trying to find my way. At the mirror, I must have touched my fingers to the smears of blood on my face, and I must have seen where the skin had been torn way from the heels of my hands.

Francie tells me that my voice, calling her from inside the bath- room, through the shut door, sounded pitiful. I said, "I need your help."

When she got out of bed to find out what was wrong, she saw the blood, and she asked me what had happened.

I told her, "I did something stupid."

My vague mumbling made it seem that I had gotten mugged, or beaten up, while doing something I was now ashamed to confess.

Then, I asked *her* what had happened. This question frightened her more than the blood. It meant my brain was out of whack.

She needed to get dressed and to find someone to stay with the girls while she took me to the emergency room for a neurological work-up. At the very least they would stitch my forehead. As for the severity of the damage to my brain, even a physician with Francie's neurological training could only guess. My loss of memory and impaired thinking might be temporary, or I might be suffering from a more serious injury with these and other permanent effects. The symptoms at the moment might be the primary phase of a response to a trauma, with life-threatening phases to come.

The injury to my brain might require immediate surgical repair. I might have had a stroke. I might have a tumor. When Francie's stepmother was in her twenties her first husband died from brain cancer within weeks of the appearance of the earliest symptoms. My own father had died more recently from three tumors in his brain.

Francie sat me down in a chair and asked me to wait while she got ready. Every time she left me there and tried to do something else, I would get up and follow her, dripping a trail of blood and asking her what was going on.

I cannot remember this. I cannot remember losing consciousness, or coming to. I remember nothing about walking home that night, being home at the time I am describing or, later, leaving for the hospital. I cannot remember getting stitched, or bandaged. Francie tells me that during this whole process, I remembered her and the children, but I did not remember much of our lives.

Two weeks earlier I had driven all night on the interstate. In a strange city an hour before dawn, I had stood over Isaac where he lay unconscious in a hospital bed with an IV in his arm. He had meningitis, they told me, a viral strain. They had done a spinal tap. With a virus, it was unlikely that he would die, they said. Bacterial meningitis is more deadly. But viral meningitis can kill people too. It can cause deafness, seizures, and brain damage. I discovered a few days later that their diagnosis was incorrect, that things were worse than they said.

Isaac was a grown man with a few days' growth of beard. I wanted to lift him in my arms and cradle his aching head in the nook of my shoulder, the way I did when he had chicken pox at four. The fear I felt at his bedside, a fear as raw as any I have ever felt, vanished from my memory the instant I hit my head. Most of my life disappeared.

❀

WHEN A POKER player represents his cards by betting, he celebrates our shared faith in deception. As Magritte reminds us in his caption: This is not a pipe. The representation is not the thing. The awareness of treachery in representation is part of our pleasure. Meanwhile we seek in treachery a sense of truth, because we understand that truth is fiction. We say that we construe the truth, or we construct it from the evidence.

Everything we know is what neurologists call representation. Anywhere we turn, an elaborate representation forms in the brain. A man looks at a photograph of his son. The lens of the eye focuses this image on the retina as a pattern of light. Cells in the retina respond to the light by translating chemical changes into neurological impulses which travel through the optic nerve to hundreds of millions of cells in the primary visual cortex at the back of the brain.

The primary visual cortex, in turn, *represents* the pattern of impulses as neuronal firings forwarded to secondary cortical areas, which generate more firings to represent spatial arrangement, contour, color, movement, binocular disparity, object recognition, and so on.

Inside the brain, this image is an unspeakably intricate network of neuronal firings. No one can picture the patterns precisely. But Isaac's face when I see the photograph in my study looks perfectly clear, although no optical image of him ever appears in my brain. There is no magic lantern in there, nothing like a lens, nor any screen where any optics can occur. Optics happen only in the eye. But in the neuronal firings, somehow, I see Isaac, and I feel my love for him.

Because perception occurs in the brain at a certain distance in space and time from the object perceived and from the sensory organs, my perception of Isaac's face is a memory even when he and I are together. But we are not together. Any memory, any scrap of love I ever know, will have to be a pattern of neuronal firings. From reading about this, I conclude that technical knowledge about the brain makes experience more and more deeply mysterious.

For the truly sad-sack disposition, $800,000 confiscated is a tiny object in the foreground of an enormous perspective of loss, and in the depths of that perspective the mind itself and its possessor hang on the verge of oblivion. Since 2006, when Isaac's brain and mine were hanging us a little closer to the verge than usual, my sense of the connection between us has felt stronger.

❊

AFTER SEEING ME for a few seconds at the bathroom mirror, Francie could not have helped getting ahead of herself. After an hour, when my mental status had not improved, her speculations must have felt less out of place and more distinct. After five hours without improvement, she knew that my symptoms still might vanish. This was the best and greatest likelihood. On the other hand, there was the chance my symptoms might grow worse.

No one with her knowledge of the brain could have avoided thinking about the probability of my needing surgery, as soon as possible, or about the more distant future. None of my memories which had vanished, and none of my ability to form new memories, might ever return. None of the continuity, none of the understanding of what happens in any of our lives, might ever again be possible for me. My disability might be a defining presence in Miriam's and Lillie's coming of age.

Improbabilities, which no one had considered before, swooped up suddenly into view as likelihoods, the care I might require, the surgeries and other treatments, the nursing, my inability to work, the reconfiguration of our marriage. Francie could not help thinking about these things, although I do not believe that any of these problems had yet entered my mind.

✳

FOR ME, EVERYTHING about the workings of my brain, memory in particular, has long been a mystery. But one of the most mysterious memories I have ever formed is that of the peculiar moment before dawn, when my short-term memory began to persist again beyond a minute into the longer term, six hours after I hit my head.

The first thing I remember is the moment of looking up at the images on the light panels across the room from me. It feels now, in my memory, almost as though my consciousness was surfacing from sleep. But I was not waking up. I was not groggy. My head was clear, but I did not know where I was. I could not remember having seen these scans before, but I guessed at once that they showed my own brain. I was looking at them to see if there was a spot visible anywhere. I was absorbed in my search, but I felt eerily undisturbed to be doing this, in a room which appeared to be a clinic or a hospital. I looked down at my hands, and I was surprised to find that they were heavily bandaged. The bandages were strangely thick and white. There was a nurse in the room. I was seeing her, it seemed to me, for the first time.

When I turned to Francie, I felt unsurprised to find that she was there, although I did not remember her having been there until then. I asked, "What happened?" and the nurse rolled her eyes, which I found odd.

I was not picturing myself as I appeared to her and to the doctors, a late, middle-aged man, disheveled, in torn clothes, needing a haircut and a shave. My colleague would have said that I looked like a poet. I looked like a poet who had just thrown himself from a moving car into a gutter.

I did not know that the nurse was rolling her eyes because she had heard me ask this same question every three minutes for some hours: "What happened?"

Francie answered gently, not impatiently, but with a distinct weariness in her tone. I did not know that we had been awake all night, that this was our fifth hour in the emergency room. I did not know the time of day. She had probably answered this question more than fifty times, but my whole memory of being here was of the moment that had just arrived.

A young neurologist, whom I did not recognize, but who seemed to recognize me, came into the room and started asking questions. I did not remember that the residents and the attending physician had already asked these questions. "What year is it?"

I found it insulting to be treated as though my brain did not work properly. But I could not answer. It perplexes me now that I still remember the precise details of how my brain was working when it could not yet recover huge parts of my memory.

I said, "I don't know." I was humiliated.

"What's the season?"

I should know this, I thought.

"It's cool outside," I said.

But I did not know why I thought that it was cool. I had no memory of being outside. I had a vaguely ambient impression of the air around the building, although I could not remember what building this was. I tried to picture branches on the trees, and nothing came to mind. We were in a windowless room, far from any door. In fact, I learned later, it *was* cool outside. I was wearing a long-sleeve shirt over my T-shirt. Maybe this had been my clue. But my impression that it was cool may have had nothing to do with fact. In any case, I thought, it must be spring, or fall. I felt that my teaching was in progress, though I had no memory of what courses I was teaching, or to whom. I find it very strange now that I remember these events as they appeared to my mind in the absence of much of my memory. For no particular reason, I guessed that it was spring. Maybe I was guessing from people's clothes.

No one told me it was fall, 2005.

"Who's the president?"

I remembered that Jimmy Carter was no longer in office, and I said so. My feelings about him when I said his name struck me as nostalgic. But I could not remember who had beaten him in the election. Whoever won was no longer president, I believed. That was long ago. How long, I had not the vaguest idea. No one asked me this, but I doubt that I could have guessed how old I was. Francie looks many years younger than she is, and this might have thrown me if I tried to guess.

I thought that there had been another president since Carter's successor, another president whose last name started with a C, someone from the South, and that the current president was someone else again, someone I disliked intensely. But I did not remember his name or face, or anything else about him. I could not remember my fury at his incompetence, and at the incompetence of his administration while hundreds of people were dying a few weeks earlier from the effects of Hurricane Katrina.

I felt distinctly that almost everything I used to know lay out of reach. My disability was more pungent because I was steadily working to assess, as well as I could, exactly how my thinking was impaired. My reasoning ability was there, but I could not call up the information needed for my usual paths of thought. I was humiliated by not knowing things. Claiming to know things, despite skepticism about the value of objective knowledge, is a crucial perversity in my sense of who I am. Now, I wanted to compensate. The doctor seemed to find my state of mind somewhat interesting, but not particularly. I could see that Francie empathized with my frustration, but I could also see that she was working on her diagnosis. I felt diminished.

I told the doctor, "I remember some things."

"What?" the doctor asked.

I wondered, for an instant, what I had meant. "I remember poems," I heard myself saying, "like the beginning of *Four Quartets*." Without prompting, I began to recite:

Time present and time past
Are both perhaps present in time future,
And time future contained in time past.
If all time is eternally present
All time is unredeemable.
What might have been is an abstraction
Remaining a perpetual possibility
Only in a world of speculation.

"That's good," the doctor said. He may have been cutting me off. Francie was giving me a look. She must have known, when she heard me say these eight lines, that I could keep going like this for hours. I am the only person I know who has memorized the whole of *Four Quartets*, over a thousand lines, which it takes more than an hour to recite. She was hoping that I would stop. The persistence of my memory of *Four Quartets*, especially if I kept volunteering to recite, might not have been, for her, good news. But I guessed, from her slightly apologetic amusement, that the recitation did, at least, seem promising. Maybe I was starting to come around.

I found it difficult to read the flatness of the doctor's tone, but what he said made me feel childish. Maybe he thought I was reciting gobble-dygook. I used to think that T. S. Eliot was trying to sound inscrutable when he made these lines so thoroughly abstract. I thought that he was showing off. Now I was showing off, as Francie's expression seemed to register. I do not recite, usually, to anyone who has not expressed a particular interest in poetry.

Maybe to the doctor it sounded crazy for me to be reciting for no reason, especially to be reciting this. Or maybe he thought that I was making it up, that it wasn't really a poem. He might have thought that I was complaining, arguing that my broken memory did not matter, because the present is eternal and the past is unredeemable. I might have been telling him, in anger at my disability, that you do not have to be a brain surgeon to understand the human condition. With mandarin tact, and with rude disinhibition, both at once, I might have meant to imply that my philosophical insight put the triviality of his questions to shame. Probably, I remembered this passage because it addressed my anxiety about the sudden disconnection from my past. What I meant by saying this out loud, in fact, I do not know. I said these lines because they happened to come into my head. I still find it odd that they did.

※

A FEW WEEKS earlier, Francie and I had dropped off the girls at summer camp and picked up Isaac on our way to Cape Cod. He had just finished a research project at school. Two days later Zoe took the ferry from Boston, where she lived, and we met her on the pier in Provincetown. They had been seeing each other for about six months.

At the seafood restaurant that evening, Zoe was ready to laugh, and she enjoyed herself, though she was being careful with first impressions. She loved food, which is always a good sign. She liked good books, and she made lively conversation. She told us she was enjoying her work in the theater in Boston.

She did not know us well enough to say, as she would years later, that she had been struggling with her role in a poorly written farce, a fringe production in a small, slightly rundown theater which was an oven under the lights. By the time of dress rehearsals in early July, Zoe had stopped thinking that her romance with the playwright and director had any promise. She no longer thought that he was very good at what he did. At rehearsals he started blaming the actors for problems that were caused by weaknesses in his writing. The cast responded by asking each other, in whispers, if the writing was as bad as they thought.

Now that Isaac had entered Zoe's life, and the playwright-slash-director had hooked up with another member of the cast, Zoe was the brunt of repeated attacks. Her performance, everyone soon understood, was deficient wherever it differed from that of the director's ex, who had created the part onstage the year before. To solve this problem, he kept demanding that Zoe do her lines again, in response to more and more opaque direction.

He tried teaching her to walk. He sashayed across the stage with a swing in his hips. Zoe kept a straight face, and she walked in again. Finally, he blurted, "No! That's wrong. You're not doing it like she did." Zoe understood this. It was clear, to do what he was asking, she would need to be clairvoyant, and derivative. It also seemed necessary to re-arouse his past infatuation and to make him feel that she was smitten with him too. None of these challenges interested her.

Unsurprisingly, the review of the opening in the *Globe* that next week said that the writing lacked the "inner logic" required by farce. The reviewer did, however, appreciate the cast's "game" effort to "transform the material." One of the cast, who happened to be Zoe's

roommate, left a copy of this review in the coat pocket of the direc-
tor-slash-playwright. He would be sure to appreciate, she thought, the
reviewer's judgment, that "one standout" in the cast was Zoe Weingart,
who brought "genuine charm to her role as the ditzy film star."

Zoe was being too careful about first impressions to go into any of
this at our first meeting. I might have been more careful myself. I might
have smiled and let it pass when Isaac mentioned that he brought along
some good weed. Instead, I perked right up and told him I would love
to try it. Francie said that she would not and gave me a dubious look.
By now we were back at the cottage we were renting. She reminded me
that I needed to walk Woofy and Wags before I came to bed, and she
disappeared into our bedroom.

I knew what Isaac was describing would be stronger than any
weed in my experience. Isaac and Zoe were used to it, but I was no
longer used to marijuana of any kind, much less to what the experts
were designing in the twenty-first century. I did not articulate this to
myself, but I wanted to be close to Isaac, the way we had been close
when he was a boy. I must have believed that getting stoned again the
way I did when I was his age would help close some of the distance
I felt opening between us, now that he was a grown man making his
own way out into the world.

After three puffs each, Isaac put away his fancy bubbler, and I
got the leashes. Woofy and Wags are shaggy half-breeds, dropped by
a poodle after her dalliance with a border collie. These are famously
intelligent breeds, but at the moment, they looked slightly goofy, like
something out of Dr. Seuss.

Usually, when I get the leashes, Wags comes in close, sits, and
lowers his head calmly to get his collar fastened. Woofy stands back

wagging her tail so hard that her whole body arcs back and forth, which makes her do a little dance on her forepaws. Francie calls this the three-part wiggle. Unless I grip her collar, when I lean in to fasten the leash, she springs for joy and bumps her nose hard into my face. She acts more border-collie-ish than Wags.

That night, when I found the leashes and looked up, both dogs were checking me out from across the room. The dubiousness of their expressions reminded me of the look Francie had given me before she went upstairs, except that the dogs were less amused. I was reading their minds. I narrated for Isaac and Zoe.

"Woofy cannot believe that I am this fucked up and that I plan to take her for a walk. Look at her." Isaac and Zoe laughed. "Help!" I said, in my Woofy voice, which is five tones higher than my human voice. "Save me from this maniac!" The dogs were considering whether to hide or make a break for it, but there was nowhere to go. I found them hilarious. I had never been more stoned in my life. There was a kind of transparency and lightness to the high, which felt very different from the heavier, more sedating dreaminess of the good shit Richard brought home from Asia, the strongest I had smoked before this.

Outside, the darkness was amazing. There was no moon, and no streetlight, so we made our way on the sandy road along the bay very slowly. It was a mild, clear night, and I kept looking up at the stars and stumbling. My attempts at conversation were as clumsy as my feet, but we had to stay out until the dogs had finished their business.

Isaac and Zoe did not say much, but they seemed to agree with the dogs that it was risky for me to be navigating the world in my condition. After a few hundred yards, when both the dogs were done, I was ready for bed. Still, I wanted to look at the sky a little more before we went inside.

In the galactic haze straight overhead was the constellation of the Swan, one of my favorites. Halfway down the great arc toward the east, wonderfully bright and red in the constellation of the Golden Ram, was the planet Mars. Across the calm bay, now at high tide, over the horizon of dunes—dunes heaped there by starlit glaciers ten thousand years before—the constellation of Orion the Hunter was vaulting out of the Atlantic. The photons entering our eyes from the brightest stars in Orion had been traveling across the Milky Way since before the days when Chaucer, himself a student of the heavens, said his poems out loud at court. My mind was spinning off in all directions.

Mars had been getting brighter, closer to Earth, and more fully lit from our vantage, since it began to appear in the dawn sky the previous winter, when Isaac and Zoe had started seeing each other. Two years before, it had been even brighter, brighter, maybe, than it had appeared since long before the glaciers made the Cape.

"That's Mars," I said, finding that I could hardly speak.

Zoe said, politely, "Is it?" She and Isaac looked, politely, in that general direction. There was no mistaking, even for me, that they had little interest in Mars. Furthermore, this red spot might not be Mars. Even if it were, its brightness would have no effect on anything that mattered. I lurched back one step suddenly to steady myself. I looked down at the dogs, who were worrying, with good reason, that I might fall on them. I can enjoy the night sky better when my brain is working.

Now, to recover my social balance, I wanted to tell a joke about Orion the Hunter, who had been walking his dogs, the Lead Dog and the Big Dog, all day and all night for thousands of years, and had not yet fallen. But Isaac and Zoe were already looking a little worried about me, and a joke would have required mental coordination far beyond my reach.

Instead, I asked them, "How long am I going to keep getting more and more stoned?"

Isaac said, "Oh. I think this is probably it."

It had not occurred to me that Zoe and Isaac were taking me for a walk, or that my half-baked plan to close the gap between us was itself a joke. But my brain was working well enough to know that it was time to lay my body flat before I hurt myself.

⁂

MY NAMESAKE, SAMUEL Brooks, took a Puritan's view of dancing. His daughters, sobbing in their bedroom after he forbade them to attend the ball, may have come to share his insight, as he hoped. Faces in the portraits of his kin from those days are impressively grim. Despite this inherited disposition, I like to think of myself as playful.

So, when I needed to leave the car at the shop after Francie had gone to bed, instead of walking the mile and a half back home, I thought it might be good for me to use my daughter's kick scooter.

I had seen people in Manhattan use kick scooters, ladies in their thirties with sensible shoes. Grown-up scooters were a fad. I was feeling playful when I laid Miriam's scooter in the trunk of the car and left for the shop. Then, suddenly, I was looking at CT scans on the light screens in the emergency room.

After my memory started coming back, Francie made a follow-up appointment, and the neurologist released me from the hospital. The first thing I did when we got home was to inspect the bloody scooter.

I could see what had happened. I found in the middle of the handle-
bars the ridge which must have opened the gash on my forehead. It
was clear from the torn skin on my knuckles and on the heels of my
hands that I had fallen forward with both hands squeezing the grips.
Probably, my reflex from years of riding bikes had been to squeeze the
grips when I wanted to stop.

Though I was very sore, with badly skinned knees and hands, and
raw spots on one shoulder and one elbow, I walked the route between
the repair shop and home, both ways, scanning the ground to see if I
could find the spot where I lost consciousness. Maybe my glasses, or
what was left of them, would still be where they fell. Maybe I would
see a scuffed spot or a bloodstain on the sidewalk or the road. Maybe
standing in that spot would bring back what had happened.

I walked to the repair shop scanning the sidewalk, and I walked
home scanning the road. I remembered nothing. The world on this
stretch of road felt to me uncanny, as though it had been emptied. It
retains that aura, after six years.

Francie worried that a cerebral event might have occurred before
the accident. It might have caused the accident. In an earlier stage, it
might have made scootering look sensible.

My father, a few years before, had had a series of hallucinations
and fainting spells, which the doctors identified as the effects of tran-
sient ischemic attacks. After he saw a bottomless hole in the yard, he
described it to me, in the middle of an otherwise rational conversation,
as though it had been real. The opening of this abyss still seemed to
him a curious event rather than a clear impossibility. As with me, his
brain scans revealed nothing. Two years later, the doctors found three
brain tumors, which killed him within weeks. Rather than accept the

likelihood that I too might have lesions, I preferred a more whole-heartedly genetic hypothesis. In the exercise of judgment, the executive centers in the healthy forebrain of the son of a unicyclist are playfully disposed toward scootering.

*

NO ONE HAS ever suggested that Isaac was suffering from a cerebral event when he committed his winnings to Neteller instead of leaving them in his PokerStars casino account, where they would have been safe. Everyone agrees: he got unlucky.

Four years after that bad luck, he left a comparable sum in his casino account instead of moving it. This time the Department of Justice shut down the casino. His legitimate winnings once again were snatched away. Arguably, this time, he might have known better. He might have removed a large part of this sum into a regular bank or made a more conventional investment. He was one of thousands of players caught off-guard, not by a long shot the one who lost the most.

But in August 2006, I was afraid he might be on the verge of losing a great deal more than a million dollars. He might be losing everything. I might be losing him. In a drugged and fevered sleep, afraid that he might die, Isaac kept pressing the button for the morphine pump on his IV. In his nightmares, he was feeling pain in his head. Though he has told me what he can remember, I cannot imagine what was happening in his mind.

Anyone with a vivid sense of dreams finds it impossible to describe them. Memory misrepresents our dreams even before language can misrepresent the memory. The brain keeps making one illusion after another, in dream, in memory, in language. The mind forms images as various as imagination, yet precise, in different ways, as any microscope. Whatever we remember or perceive or think, whether the brain is well or ill or injured, consciousness keeps seeking further consciousness and finding it, preoccupied at every step, even in sleep, with intimations of what is.

All action in the mind is predicated on a wager like Pascal's, because the thing itself, like God, is out of reach. We wager that the mind is showing us what matters. We do this on the strength of probabilities. You could call the pot at stake in this game *truth*, the way my mother did, or you could call it *being*. *Ultimate being*, you could call it, whether or not that being is *supreme*.

✻

NOT LONG AFTER we met Zoe on the Cape, when Isaac told us on the phone about his headache, the stiffness in his neck, and his sensitivity to light, we made him promise to get his friends to take him to the emergency room. What he was describing was the classic presentation of meningitis.

From the spinal tap, the doctors concluded it was meningitis, a viral strain. They released him with pills to relieve his headache. But he kept throwing up the pills, and the pain kept getting worse. We insisted again the next day, over his objections, that he return to the hospital, where they could give him IV drugs which would relieve the headache, lessen the nausea, and replenish the fluids he was losing. We told him that avoiding permanent ill effects from the illness might depend on getting to the hospital right away. What scared us most was that the symptoms had kept getting worse.

Francie and I drove overnight with Miriam and Lillie. We arrived in Providence before dawn, as luck would have it, at Miriam Hospital.

Zoe, whom Francie and I had met on Cape Cod three weeks earlier, was sitting beside Isaac's bed, in the dimly lighted room. Even with IV medication Isaac's headache was excruciating, and his nausea and photophobia were persistent. The nurses were treating the symptoms and waiting for the infection to pass. Over the next few days, Francie found it impossible to contact the doctors responsible for the treatment plan, to verify the logic of the diagnosis or their choices in response.

The most redeeming thing about this time was to see Zoe's steady, loving attention to Isaac when he was sick. Francie's vigilance, of course, was nothing new.

Under morphine, Isaac was having three recurrent dreams.

In one, he sits at a poker table with a draw for a straight. He calculates the odds. Hand after hand, the flop keeps leaving him with outs for a straight. He keeps figuring his odds, over and over. It makes him queasy. The anxiety in the dream feels more urgent than an actual game. It feels to him like worrying he will die.

I stood over Isaac's bed, where he kept mumbling, from the fever and the pain. I felt more helpless than I did when night terrors struck him at the age of four or when his fever from chicken pox rose to 106. All of us were terrified, and things were worse than we knew. We did not know yet that the virus was inside his brain.

In the second dream, Isaac is running on the moon. The planet Earth is in the night sky. He keeps stumbling by earthlight over a desert littered with disgusting corpses. They keep tripping him, as if on purpose. A nightmare beast is stalking him. It has instead of a head only a huge mouth gaping with long fangs, and instead of a body only a neck. It runs on haunches like those of the theropods he feared as a boy. Everything about this dream has all the legendary vividness for which the opiates are famous.

Isaac recognizes the creature from a black card in the Magic deck, where it has the name Flesh Reaver. The black cards are associated with illness and death. In the dream, Isaac has to keep moving as fast as he can to stay away from the Reaver. He feels nauseated in disgust at the corpses. The effort to lift his feet is grindingly tedious, but he is afraid to stop.

Isaac's childhood wonder at the beauty of the moon and his fear of theropods make this dream for me the most horrific. The third dream I find less disturbing, but Isaac tells me that this one troubled him the most. He stands in an empty white space, like the one where Morpheus explains to Neo in *The Matrix* that the world he thinks he knows is in fact an illusion generated in a computer.

In this white emptiness, which they call the Construct, Isaac stands with a beautiful woman in a black dress. She has pale skin and dark straight hair. She holds an empty wine glass and Isaac holds a bottle of wine. He is about to pour wine into her glass, and he feels self-conscious because he wants very much to please her, and he knows that he will fail. He starts to pour the wine. He wants to avoid spilling. But he spills. He feels humiliated and angry at himself. Something somewhere feels more deeply wrong. This dream, like the others, plays over and over again.

In the waking world, Francie and Zoe sit on either side of Isaac's bed. Lillie, Miriam, and I appear and disappear. The six of us all wait.

Isaac feels that he cannot escape being the person in the dreams. Yet at the same time, he keeps watching that person helplessly from a distance.

From a greater distance now I try to understand. The Flesh Reaver, like Isaac's illness, threatens death. The strangeness of the Reaver's necklike body represents the stiffness in Isaac's neck. A being with no head pursues him while he wishes that the pain in his own head would disappear. His nausea on the moon, exhaustion, remove from the world of the living, and nearness to the unliving are not very far from the literal facts. This interpretation seems straightforward.

The third dream I find more elusive. The sunglasses Isaac borrowed from his roommate when the photophobia set in might have reminded him of Neo. Neo is famous for his shades.

The woman's black outfit, dark hair, and pale complexion make her look like Trinity, Neo's lover, who, just before the scene in the Construct, has inserted a long metal probe into a socket at the base of his brain, so that they can upload into him the programs that reveal the Matrix and the Construct. This input prong resembles the huge needle they just used to tap Isaac's spine. Now, a smaller needle in Isaac's arm was supplying morphine (the elixir of the dream-god, Morpheus). Isaac's phobia about needles may account for the suppression of these details in the dream and for some of the fear he finds mysterious.

It makes sense that a student beginning to feel trapped in his computer science program might dream of himself as a character trapped and paralyzed by computers, and that a student of Latin, who knows the word *matrix* from *mater* for mother, might dream about a Matrix while his mother sat beside his bed.

To go with the standard Freudian sense of the wine bottle and the glass as emblems of sexual anxiety about wanting to please a woman feels plausible, but insipid. More to the point, I think, the hospital room was a kind of white space like the Construct, a whiteness made overwhelming by photophobia. This place was *his* room. His visitors made this a social situation in which he as host would be obliged to pour. The problem outside the dream was not mere presentation of wine, but the presentation of his new life-partner Zoe to his mother, and of his mother to Zoe. He wanted to please them both, as any son and lover would. The Trinity, whom Isaac, paralyzed by illness and morphine, could not serve, would seem to be the trinity of Francie, Zoe, and himself.

❋

ANY REPRESENTATION OF a dream confuses fact and fiction. The confusion is already there in the tangled memory of dreams when we awaken. Twenty-five hundred years ago, Chuang Tzu wrote that he dreamed he was a butterfly, and when he woke to find that he was Chuang Tzu, he wondered if he might really be a butterfly dreaming that he was Chuang Tzu.

As for me, I could not help much twenty years ago, when I tried to understand night terrors, and I cannot help much now by trying to understand opium dreams. Still I resist the fact that I cannot be in Isaac's dreams to help when he needs help.

He was relieved, in any case, to awaken outside the Construct of Morpheus, god of dreams, even if it was only to find himself in a hospital room, which was the Construct of Asklepios, god of healers. He was lucky to be alive. What were the odds?—for the six of us all to have found our way this far, to be together, thankfully, in one place in such a web of memories and dreams. We were unbelievably lucky. We still are, though I feel superstitious saying so.

After three days, Isaac went from sucking queasily on ice cubes to being able to drink and eat without throwing up. Zoe and Francie were punch-drunk by then, cracking up at the sight of Isaac in his borrowed sunglasses shuffling with his IV pole from bed to toilet and back. Without having heard about the dreams of Neo, they agreed that Isaac looked ridiculously like Nic Cage in *Leaving Las Vegas*. They were laughing from exhaustion and relief, to see the man they loved alive and on the mend, moving under his own steam.

The less morphine Isaac took, the more he complained about the sores on his back. The day we were leaving, Francie noticed that the rash had erupted in a pattern associated with nerve endings around the lower spinal column. This kind of rash is a sign of varicella zoster infection, the virus that produces chicken pox. The dermatomal rash suggested that Isaac's illness was not only meningitis, but encephalitis as well, the full-blown brain infection that tends to come when varicella attacks the central nervous system.

The virus, which hit Isaac hard on our vacation in Saint Lucia, stayed for fifteen years in the ganglia of his lower back. It can stay that way without producing symptoms of infection for sixty years or more. The resurgence of the infection usually comes, if ever, under stress or in old age, when the immune system is less robust, so that the peculiar construction of the virion, which is not a life form but a kind of undead protein particle, compels its living host to reconstruct it in great numbers. This proliferation of millions of unliving agents constructed by the living host is so much like the swarming of robots in *The Matrix* that I find Isaac's dream uncannily precise.

The second outbreak in most people is a case of shingles. More rarely, very rarely in a healthy young adult, it may infect the brain and spinal fluid. The immunological quirk which made Isaac's chicken pox so severe probably made him more highly vulnerable to the second infection.

In any case, the attending on his rounds told Francie, when she confronted him, that what she showed him was not a dermatomal rash. He said it was a case of bedsores. Bedsores do not even vaguely resemble the pustules of a dermatomal rash, and the pattern here was so distinct that it could have been a textbook illustration. But the doctor kept a poker face. He did not revise the diagnosis. No one could have been this thoroughly oblivious. His job, as he saw it at that point, was to try to diminish the probability of a lawsuit.

We were grateful that the hospital had treated Isaac's pain and replenished his fluids and nutrients when he could not eat or drink. Mainly, we were grateful to the mysterious powers of probability, that he was alive and well. Now, the odds would be better if he got away from the hospital before someone made a more serious blunder. We drove home as soon as we could, the six of us still together, to let him rest a few days before school started.

Francie, meanwhile, ordered further tests on the spinal fluid in the lab, and her diagnosis was confirmed. Although she avoids a game whenever she can, Francie might be said again to have played one well. But medical school, in my opinion, is a form of cheating.

SIN CITY

where
LOVERS have been *LOST*
and *FOUND*
according to the LAWS
of NUMBER
and
the LOVING HEART

ISAAC AND ZOE were staying at the fanciest honeypot on the Strip, but they were in no mood to celebrate. The poker circuit was a grind. Zoe was down with the flu, and Isaac had just busted out of a tournament in San Jose. Meanwhile, his winnings from the Caribbean Adventure had been held by the Department of Justice for two months, and his confidence that he would see the money again was shakier than ever. He had decided to sell half of his action in upcoming tournaments, so that he could still afford the entry fees.

Now, at two-thirty in the morning, there was a party on the hotel roof to witness the destruction of the Stardust Tower across the street. The festivities outside their window sounded like the Fourth of July. They could see fireworks. They could feel the detonation and collapse. But they could not see the tower coming down, and they did not care.

The implosion might have interested them if they knew that they would be living nearby for three years, or that the earliest history of the neighborhood had brought Isaac's family there.

❀

A FEW HUNDRED yards from where they slept that night, El Rancho had opened as the first hotel and casino on Highway 91 south of what was then a little-known desert town. Eight months later the Japanese bombed Pearl Harbor. The following year, during the gala opening for the Last Frontier, the United States was fighting the largest war in history. The Last Frontier was not the first hotel and casino on that stretch of road, but it was fancier than its predecessor. The following summer, when my Aunt Anna sat with her baby in the shade beside the Frontier pool and my mother swam and read a book, Allied troops were sweeping north from Sicily and landing at Salerno and Taranto. Hundreds of thousands had died in the fighting, and millions more would soon be dying.

The baby's father was on training maneuvers with the Ninth Armored Division in the desert at Needles, California, a hundred miles away. Saturdays on leave, he would spend as much time as he could with his wife, who had traveled fifteen hundred miles in a sweltering car to let him hold his daughter a few times before he took his chances in the war. None of the men in the division knew that they would be landing at Normandy within a year and fighting in the Battle of the Bulge.

While the desert heat climbed well into the hundreds, Ava Gardner, like the dozens of Army wives in the shade of umbrellas by the pool, was trying to chill. She was twenty, a few months younger than my mother, and as beautiful, they say, as any major star in Hollywood, though she would not become a star until after the war, when she played Burt Lancaster's sultry, double-crossing girlfriend in *The Killers*.

The deferential young man in a suit and tie who visited Gardner every day beside the pool was paid by Howard Hughes to see that she had everything she needed while she was waiting for her divorce from Mickey Rooney. Coincidentally, she was a small-town Southern girl like my mother, but already she had transformed herself into the image of youth's infinite possibility.

The difference between Ava Gardner and my mother, or between my mother and the young widows-to-be who had gathered beside the pool, was the luck of the draw.

※

SOME OF WHAT I know about my mother's first stay in Las Vegas comes from an essay in her last collection of nonfiction. Her career as a publishing writer started when she was forty, and her first novella appeared in *The New Yorker*. For the next forty years, her work, written under the pen name Ellen Douglas, kept earning prizes and unanimous praise from reviewers.

At the threshold of adulthood, in 1943, she felt her calling as a writer more distinctly when she read Proust in the shade of an umbrella by the Frontier pool. In his work, she saw what she called "that grandest of all illusions, the landscape of the imagination, where the artist dreams that he will always be at home."

She danced on Saturday nights with whichever soldier my Uncle Jim had brought along as her blind date. She was a beautiful girl, lately in the homecoming court at Ole Miss, and she would have tried to be good company to any boy in uniform. But her first love had broken her heart, and she still felt the pangs too much, I think, to take a genuine interest in someone new. Her essay does not mention this. She does say she was ill at ease with her blind dates.

The first time I heard my mother speak the name of Norman Dowty, I laughed. *Norman* sounded like a dork, like Alfred E. Newman. *Dowty* reminded me of Howdy Doody. I must have been ten, and my mother told me not to laugh at that name, ever. I could see, after she snapped at me, that she was reading from my face how strange her voice had sounded. I thought she might be on the verge of tears. I had never seen her look at me this way.

She and Norman Dowty, I learned in my teens, were high school sweethearts. They broke things off before the war. He had just come back from an adventure, working in Alaska, and now, he told her, he wanted to ride the rails, to see the country as a hobo. That was the only way he could afford to travel, not that he was complaining. She said, if he lit out again, he could forget about her waiting for him. He said OK and caught a freight. When I was ten and wondering if she would cry, the freight had left town almost twenty years before.

She told me the story when I was a college sophomore, hitchhiking around the country just because I could. Norman, she said, was a good-looking Irish boy, intelligent and dashing, with a sense of humor, a war-hero-to-be. The warmth of her description made me think about the differences between Norman, enlisting after Pearl Harbor, and me, taking a student deferment after Tet.

❊

MY BROTHER AYRES and his wife stopped in Las Vegas on their way to see Richard in California not long after he had bought a house there. They were traveling with my mother and her best friend, the four of them in a van Ayres had bought for taking bikes on the racing circuit. To make room for the passengers on this trip, they left the racing bikes behind and put their clothes in an old chest of drawers tied to the braces in the side wall of the cargo area. This meant that instead of luggage, when they checked into the hotel in Las Vegas, Ayres was carrying two dresser drawers.

The hotel reminded him of his favorite story about Las Vegas, which he told my mother after he had set the drawers on a chair by the check-in counter. When he started racing, he said, Bart Markel was establishing his all-time record for the most American Motorcyclist Association Grand National wins. Markel was older and smaller than Ayres, slight, but tough, a Golden Gloves champion, and as a racer, he had earned the nickname Black Bart by nudging his competition out of the way.

Black Bart happened to meet his favorite actor, Lee Marvin, in a hotel lobby. For his role as leader of a gang in *The Wild One*, Marvin had learned to ride, and later he tried racing, though, unlike Markel, he was too big for the sport, at six foot two. A bad boy all his life, repeatedly expelled from high school, Marvin fought as a marine sniper in the Battle of Saipan. He was lucky there only to get wounded, since most of the men in his company died in action. Back in Hollywood, he made his name as a heavy.

Black Bart, who had also served in the Marine Corps and who was, essentially, the Lee Marvin of flat-track racing, introduced himself in the hotel lobby at the edge of the casino area, and asked if his wife JoAnn could get a snapshot of two of them together. Marvin was perfect, almost too good to be true. He was as surly in person as he was on the screen. He said, "Get the fuck outta here!"

Meanwhile, there was JoAnn with her camera ready. So, when Marvin turned to walk away, Black Bart jumped up, got him into a headlock, twisted till they faced the camera, and said, "OK, honey, snap it!"—which she did, a memento of improbability.

❈

WITHIN A YEAR of joining the Navy, Norman Dowty married a girl who followed him from base to base while he trained as a pilot. His assignment to combat duty came through while my mother was staying at the Last Frontier. He flew sorties off carriers in the North Atlantic to fight U-boats, at a time when a combat pilot's life expectancy was a few months. Whether or not he saw his daughter before his squadron shipped out, I do not know.

On the morning of March 19, 1944, southwest of the Cape Verde Islands, under heavy fire, Lieutenant Junior Grade Norman Dowty and Aviation Radioman First Class Edgar Burton, aboard a Grumman TBF Avenger, dropped two depth bombs which exploded on either side of the conning tower of U-1059, sinking the boat within seconds. The plane then circled to return to the carrier, but one wing dipped, and the plane went down into the waves. Under the tropical sun that morning, the U-boat and the plane, with men on board, both sank until they stopped three miles below, where they still are, in the subzero darkness.

※

WHEN THE WAR ended, my mother, as a young housewife in Greenville, Mississippi, learned to pilot a small plane. She did takeoffs and landings and flew up and down along the winding channel of the River, but she chose not to log as many hours as she needed for the pilot's license. She told me that she never wanted a license. She just wanted to know how it felt to fly a plane. She wanted to fly low over water.

At ninety, she took to singing a song she must have learned as a little girl. Many versions of these lyrics were popular with the singing schools of the commanderies of Civil War veterans. My mother's grandmother, who liked to sing, would have learned it in her youth.

Here the boat goes round the bend,
Good-bye, my lover, good-bye,
She's loaded down with boys and men,
Good-bye, my lover, good-bye!

My mother sang the refrain, as she must have learned it in her childhood. When she sang, she said, she thought of Norman Dowty.

⁂

EVERYWHERE AND EVERYTHING and everyone we know will disappear.

While I write this sentence, Isaac and Zoe are asleep downstairs. Tomorrow they leave: a tournament in Florida, then Vancouver, for the play online, then Malta, then who knows?

We had a feast, the six of us, last night. Tonight another feast. Tomorrow, kisses at the airport by the curb.

⁂

IN ONE VIDEO of the Stardust implosion, at the edge of the frame is a neon sign for the most recent incarnation of the Last Frontier. The person with the video camera stands in the Frontier parking lot. The Stardust is just across Desert Inn Road. In place of the Desert Inn, unseen in the video, is the Wynn Las Vegas, the newest, fanciest hotel in town, where Isaac and Zoe stand at the window, brooding, over the flurry of fireworks.

Life-changing things happened in the rooms of the Stardust. People stumbled in at just this hour, because their love required attention, or they sat up through the night alone, because a lover who required attention was with someone else. A few spectators in the parking lot, and more who watch the video, must have taken one of these thousand rooms, on a reckless getaway or a honeymoon.

After the rockets die down, flares strung on the façade of the Stardust Tower form the number ten. Then, nine. The crowd in the parking lot counts down in unison with the flares, whistling and yelling. At the number one, five blue-white sparkling fountains spurt up from the roof. Then, everything goes dark, and under five high plumes of smoke, explosions sound inside.

The windows of the Stardust Tower have already been removed, but the buckling of steel and broken concrete sounds almost like shattering glass. The tower, falling in on itself and disappearing, all thirty-two stories of it, in five seconds is completely gone. For something so large to be gone so fast is uncanny, yet the whole thing seems to come down in slow motion. Air at high speed rushing through collapsing rooms and corridors makes a muffled roar mixed on the video into the sounds of shattering.

A thick plume of dust rises in a few more seconds, sucked up into a vacant shape of low air pressure left by the collapse, a cloud a little higher than the building was. This huge cloud rolls in all directions. It engulfs the palm trees in the dark along the edge of the road. When the crowd sees dust roiling toward them, everyone turns and walks away. Some look back from time to time. Someone in the crowd may think of Lot's wife looking back at Sodom and turning, suddenly, into a pillar of salt.

※

THE IMPROBABILITIES, THE contradictions, and the incompleteness experts find in math and science also work in poker, and in love.

My mother, who was nimble in her wits and full of empathy and insight, after a lifetime wrestling the most consequential truths she could set down in words, sang in terminal dementia her good-bye, "Good-bye, my lover, goodbye," but not to anyone alive.

※

IN A NEIGHBORHOOD of identical new houses at the edge of the desert, three months after the implosion, Isaac and Zoe sat with their four housemates on a pair of couches with shiny red slipcovers and no cushions, in a living room with an unpainted cinderblock wall, just inches from their window. They were renting short-term in Las Vegas during the 2007 World Series of Poker.

Alex, Isaac's friend from Magic, and Alex's fiancée were staying in one of the bedrooms, Isaac and Zoe in another. Alex did not know yet that he would win $131,000 in one of the tournaments on this trip. The others of their crew were friends from college. Scott had yet to post his first big cash, though he would win more than $4 million in the next four years. Scott was sleeping on a futon in the hall.

Sam, who has now finished putting himself through law school at Berkeley by playing poker online using skills he learned from Isaac, was staying in one of the bedrooms. But instead of playing tournaments, he had enrolled for fun in cooking classes at the University of Las Vegas.

Their friend Ben had been collecting discarded exercise equipment from various curbsides and assembling these in the yard. He was experimenting with ways to make ends meet. He had received an excellent basketball scholarship, since he was seven feet tall. Sometimes he traveled to play slot machines, if the payout schedule for the machines made it look worthwhile to keep playing one until it dumped. He hired student workers to process entry slips for sweepstakes in Connecticut, where the law required that unlimited free entries be distributed in any contest where no purchase is necessary.

On the night in question, all the housemates were together, celebrating the premier broadcast on cable of the coverage for the final table at Paradise Island. Three of them, Alex, Scott, and Zoe, had been spectators in the wind on the veranda that late afternoon.

Isaac was sharing with Zoe a bottle of Goldschläger, a colorless cinnamon schnapps with two claims to fame. One was its high alcohol content, which used to be more than a hundred proof. The other was a glitter of thinly beaten gold flakes, which flurried up like snow in a snow globe, whenever you took a swig. Isaac chose this drink in honor of the gelt he had won. By recent calculations, after a surge in the value of gold, the glitter in that bottle of Goldschläger would be worth five bucks. Since the gold and liquor altogether cost less than a mediocre bottle of bourbon, the value of the schnapps itself had to have been low. Isaac's most substantial gelt, meanwhile, had been confiscated by the Department of Justice, and no one knew what it was worth, if anything, besides a six-figure tax debt.

Isaac and Zoe were so uneasy about appearing on television that they drank Goldschläger. Isaac found that he could drink a good deal of it, fast.

His friends were teasing him, meanwhile, about his baby face in shades with long hair blowing in his eyes. They hooted with admiration at his bluff with the nut low, and without mercy, they mocked his disastrous tell and the speed with which he lost his huge advantage in the chip count.

Francie and I were watching at home in Syracuse. We saw Isaac on camera, with Zoe, Miriam, and Lillie at the rail. We heard the commentators, several times, refer to Isaac as "the poet's son." We thought this was funny. Francie said that she liked to think of Isaac as the psychiatrist's son. But the point when they mentioned my standing as a poet was not honorific. They found it droll that a card shark's father would pursue work even more improbable than his son's. Making a living as a poet is like making a living at craps. Though hypothetically possible, it cannot, in fact, be done.

＊

EIGHT MONTHS AFTER the implosion of the Stardust, if Isaac and Zoe had been at the window of the same hotel room at the same hour, they could have seen pirates on the deck of a ship at Barbary Cove, in front of Treasure Island to the south, fire their cannon at the Frontier Tower to the north. They would have seen the tower, built long after Isaac's grandmother and Ava Gardner stayed at that address, go down as though struck in the heart with an exploding round.

By this time Isaac and Zoe had left town. Isaac had been waiting six months for the decision of the court in the Neteller case. Luckily, he had not sold his account at a substantial loss, as several predatory souls suggested, because one goodhearted poker player with connections in the industry had told him what everyone on the executive grapevine was saying, that the full amount of the Neteller accounts would be returned to everyone within the year.

Finally, in July 2007, the Neteller defendants, Lawrence and Lefebvre, pleaded guilty to the charges, and in August, a check made out to Isaac for the full $800,000 arrived in the mail. The full amount did not include the $20,000 in interest, which the confiscated cash would have earned in escrow if the Department of Justice had taken a single step to protect the innocent victims of their action.

That fall, Isaac returned to school, satisfied with the results of his year off. Although he has never said a mumbling word on this subject to Francie or to me, the choice to finish school must have seemed to him more questionable than his year off. But he discourages young players from dropping out to play, because he believes that this move generates a lower expectation for most people. In any case, he returned to Brown and finished his degree in the logic and philosophy of science, while Zoe holed up in a house off campus, which they shared with Scott and Sam.

Zoe remembered why she had been glad to postpone Isaac's senior year. The university neighborhood was full of reminders. There were the places where she went when she missed classes, until she fell too far behind and dropped them. There were buildings where the drama students watched her struggle onstage, while her passion as an actor seeped away, and her technique, solid from years of study, began to feel hollow. Everywhere she went was haunted by what went wrong, in school and art and love.

At home all day, she could not seem to find the power to decide her life, and whatever was deciding things for her felt hidden, and remote. She went out less and less often. Her psychiatrist said that she was having a crisis of motivation. Her youthful spirit was burning low, and she became a person she disliked, or a nonperson. It felt histrionic to see herself this way and false to deny it.

Whenever she and Isaac talked about where they were going to live next, he said he thought Las Vegas might be good. The casinos there held more major tournaments than anywhere else. There was no local or state tax on income. The housing market there was going under, and they could get a good place cheap.

Zoe hated this idea. The place to go for theater was New York.

Isaac did not think that this was completely out of the question. But New York had high rent and taxes. Besides, though Isaac felt brutal hearing himself say so, Zoe had not done theater in more than a year. She could have been active in Boston or in Providence. It made no sense to choose a place to live for opportunities in theater, when she was no longer doing that.

One day, Isaac found her in the kitchen staring into the freezer, which was filled with baggies of unlabeled soup stock left there by Sam, who was still teaching himself to cook. She knew that there was nothing wrong with baggies of frozen broth, except to her they looked like fluid aspirated from malignancies.

Isaac was standing behind her. He spoke quietly. His carpal tunnel syndrome from hours of using the mouse to play online was hurting him, he said, and he went rummaging for Motrin in the medicine cabinet when he happened to notice that her medicine bottles were empty. He told her that her prescriptions had run out weeks before. There was already an edge to his voice. He wanted to know if she had been keeping her doctor's appointments.

She had not, but this was beside the point. Isaac was putting pressure on her. He knew, she said, that pressure made things worse.

For months Isaac had been coaxing her to take better care of herself. He had tried to be patient, to be calm and soothing. After a while, he could tell, he sounded more long-suffering than kind. This time suddenly he was telling her at the top of his voice, if this was the best that she could do for herself, he gave up. He stormed out into the back yard alone and started smashing scrap lumber into bits. Zoe watched from the window. She had never seen him like this. It scared her. She phoned a friend and left on the next available flight.

When she arrived in Santa Barbara, she was beginning to doubt that she could ever make things work for them or for herself. But once she was out walking in the sunshine under a clear sky, she felt better. With her friend she went shopping at the Farmers' Market. They cooked good food and ate together. They relaxed and talked. It was a relief, all of a sudden, to remember who she was. When she reflected on the life that she and Isaac had been putting together for three years, now that she could see it clearly from a distance, she thought that wherever the two of them were, that was the life she wanted.

After a week, she came back to Providence and told Isaac that she was ready to make things work. Las Vegas was a good place for them to go, and she wanted to help set it up. While he finished school, she found them an apartment there. A few weeks later, she was driving them cross-country west, and they were both feeling lucky again that they were together.

❋

CARDS ARE IN the air.

❋

IN LAS VEGAS, Zoe's chances of finding work as an actor were nil. She answered an ad on Craigslist for a costume mistress. The employers' place of business was their house, which was at the far end of the farthest suburb southwest, in a neighborhood of identical houses not yet five years old, where the most recent construction had suddenly halted and where foreclosed signs would soon be marking every third yard. The proprietor, a middle-aged clothing designer from Ecuador, wore tight pants which had not fit in years. His wife was more than ten years younger, in her thirties, with perfectly rigid, almost hemispherical breasts. She had been a showgirl in her day. Her face was also rigid, like a smiling mask.

Their garage was full of hundreds of costumes for showgirls, everything all glitter, with big headpieces on shelves crammed with feather boas, cigarette trays, spangled bra and panty sets, and laundry baskets full of ostrich-feather fans and silly hats. Everything was third-rate, dirty, and in poor repair. Zoe's job was to organize the inventory in heat which must have averaged more than 110 degrees. When orders came, she fetched whatever items were required. When costumes were returned, she hung them where they belonged.

Because she had no work table, Zoe spent most of her time in the living room on her hands and knees, making alterations and repairing dingy outfits with hot glue.

Her boss's mother stood behind her, clucking disapproval of the work, smoking, and speaking in rapid Spanish under her breath. Zoe felt that she was being blamed for the invention of spandex, for all instances of its abuse, for the poor quality of leopard-skin prints, and for the tawdriness of bright pink, 100 percent synthetic crepe de chine.

When Isaac went abroad to play in the European Poker Tour, Zoe was grateful that her boss promised to hold the job for her. And when she returned, she was even more grateful that they had replaced her.

✻

ONE NIGHT, IN a high-stakes poker room on the Strip, Isaac joined three card sharks in a game which had formed around a basketball star. While the card sharks were winning thousands of dollars each, the ball player made conversation with his date. He seemed not to care about the losses. But, whenever he held a promising hand, he would stop talking to his date and pay attention to the game. He might just as well have turned his cards face-up.

The basketball player might not have understood that he was playing out of his league, and none of the card sharks wished to undeceive him. He deceived his opposition for a living, too. When he drove under a well-defended hoop as if he were going in for a layup and shoveled the ball back out to his teammate standing undefended in the paint, deception was the essence of the game. The card sharks, like him, won with skill.

When the ball player left, the other card sharks, who knew each other from working the casinos in Vegas for some years, decided to keep playing until they took Isaac's share of the winnings. This was a logical business decision. Isaac looked ridiculously young, and he was probably not as skillful as they were. A moderately competent player could have done as well as Isaac had in the game so far.

The universal wisdom of the poker room is that you should look at the faces around the table, and if you cannot find the mark, you are the mark: you should stop playing at once. In this case, the consensus of the other three sharks was as clear as if they had told Isaac to his face that he was the mark. They did not bother to disguise what they were thinking any more than the basketball star had done.

In the realm of mathematical probability, however, where the game was taking place, Isaac was not the mark. After they lost for a few rounds, it was easy for them to see: they had miscalculated. They were the marks. In a life at the poker table, this kind of miscalculation is bound to happen from time to time. They decided now to go to the Spearmint Rhino and spend their winnings on lap dances and champagne instead of losing the rest to the new kid in town. They were friendly about this change in business plan and invited Isaac to come along, but he said no thanks and headed home to Zoe.

He seldom played in the casinos, because online he could play four times as many hands per hour and the rake was much lower than it was on the Strip. He played the big casinos only when he happened to find an unusually promising table.

Online, he started playing at the very highest stakes, because one of the players at that level was a billionaire, less accomplished than the pros. Soon enough, Isaac got the billionaire into a pot for a quarter of a million dollars. Isaac had flopped the nut straight against the billionaire's two pair. It was a dream scenario. Isaac figured that the billionaire was a five-to-one dog, and he was right. After the turn, the odds were ten to one in Isaac's favor. But the billionaire rivered the boat. The decisiveness of the river can be heart-wearying, whether you try to fade a heart or something else.

In four months of what they call the nosebleeds (the highest of the high-stakes games), this kind of thing happened over and over. The billionaire lost millions, as everyone expected, but not to Isaac. Isaac, meanwhile, kept losing to the top pros, though when he analyzed their play and his, he concluded that his strategy was sound and would prevail in a significant sample of hands.

Some of Isaac's friends who had bought a share of his action tried to tell him what he was doing wrong. Isaac told them, he was doing nothing wrong. It was the way the deck was running. His friends, whose money he was losing along with his own, had different ideas. One of them, down fifty grand, knocked on Isaac's door while he was sleeping. Zoe answered. Apparently, the billionaire was in a game online, and Isaac needed to play.

By the time Isaac stopped playing the nosebleeds, he had lost well over a million dollars. The odds had been in Isaac's favor, but the outcome was not. It took some months in midstakes play to make this up.

In March 2011, Isaac told me he was killing in the sit-and-goes, games where two players buy in for $1,000 each and play until one of them has won the other's chips. One game in this format took less than five minutes. Isaac was playing four tables at a time, about fifty games an hour. I asked him what he meant by *killing*. He said that he was winning 51 percent of the games. In an hour, in other words, he was winning, on average, one game more than he lost. This was killing. An edge of one in fifty games may not sound like killing, until you figure that by playing at this rate for only one hour a day, you would net, after a year, $365,000. Two years later, Isaac told me, the quality of play in these games had improved, and his edge was less.

In April 2011, internet poker was shut down in the United States. This was no surprise. Players had deposited their money in supposedly secure accounts, which one of the largest companies assured them were "held separate from our operating accounts." The company then distributed the contents of these accounts to its board and owners.

When the federal prosecutor compares this operation to a Ponzi scheme, it seems that the electronic conveyance of the money may be confusing the issue. If the casino had been securing funds, for example, in safety deposit boxes, and administrators had been obliged to remove the cash from the safety deposit boxes, using crowbars, the nature of the crime would be less confusing.

I have read that some of the accused believe that the distribution of this money does not involve a crime, that it should be considered nothing more than the failure of a poorly run business. If the people who emptied these accounts are not criminals, I congratulate them for their skill at appropriating other people's money with impunity. In that case, however, I can see no reason to think of the business as poorly run.

I would like to express my moral outrage, but, when I try to discover the moral principle whereby the *law* distinguishes between deception and dishonesty in general, I find, as I have mentioned, that there is no moral principle. Isaac is hopeful that he will recover what was wrongly taken. If he does, he will be luckier than the millions of recent investors who trusted the bundlers of loans, designers of financial instruments, and hedge-fund managers under the most elaborately deceptive circumstances in the history of finance. In the case of these deceptions, the appropriate indictments do not seem to be forthcoming.

My own morals are a fog of hedonism. To say that I resemble most of my compatriots in this respect is as close as I come to moral leadership. I prefer not to play poker for much money, because it makes my stomach hurt.

On a visit to Isaac and Zoe's apartment in Las Vegas, I watched him four-tabling online, heads up, against Peter Eastgate, the Dane who had recently won the $9 million first prize in the Main Event of the 2008 World Series of Poker. Eastgate and Isaac, both of them twenty-three at that time, bought in for $10,000 at each of the tables, and Eastgate bought in again, a few more times, at $5,000 or $10,000 a pop. They played about five hundred hands before Isaac found himself holding all the chips.

In 2010, Viktor Blom, a Swede using the screen name of Isildur1, after a year of record-breaking ups and downs in the nosebleed games, was widely regarded, at twenty years of age, as one of the strongest and most unpredictable heads-up, no-limit hold 'em players in the world. When Blom joined the ranks of the pro players associated with PokerStars, he offered to play all comers, heads-up with a buy-in of $150,000, in what he called a Superstar Showdown. The match would last until one of the players won the total buy-in or until they had played twenty-five hundred hands, four-tabling. Blom calculated that this format would minimize the possibility of a lucky win. Isaac agreed, and he was the first player in the world to sign up for a match.

I was in Syracuse watching online, Isaac was in Vegas, and Blom, I guess, was at home in Sweden. It is difficult to follow strategy in a match where most hands are folded before the turn and few are played to the point where either player shows his cards. The average duration of a hand was about twenty seconds, and there were always four hands going at a time.

Watching made my head swim. Isaac pulled ahead, then Blom, then Isaac. In the last few hundred hands, Blom's erratically large bets indicated that he had more riding on this match than the money on the table. Isaac, by exploiting these late deviations from strategic play, more than doubled his lead.

Ten other players accepted Blom's challenge, and all ten lost, an average of $70,000 each. Isaac, the only one of ten challengers to come out ahead, won $41,000. Blom thought that Isaac was a weak player who had gotten lucky. Proclaiming himself the best in the world, after about a year, he challenged Isaac to a rematch, which Isaac won as well. The second time, Blom refrained from making snide remarks in public. Isaac, meanwhile, had been even luckier in the other seventy-five hundred hands he played against Blom in cash games online, winning more than six times as much again. Twelve thousand five hundred hands is not a large enough sample to be statistically reliable as a measure of which of two players is definitively better, but international odds makers gave Isaac the edge when they played in a third Superstar Showdown for higher stakes, for $500,000. Isaac felt that he was playing well, but Blom won back in this one game more than he had lost in the others.

✳

BECAUSE THE LOGIC of our understanding contradicts itself, and because everything the mind commemorates has already disappeared into the past before we understand it, enlightenment is said by some to be spontaneous and infinite delight in nothingness as the ground and essence of our being.

Shuffle up and deal.

✳

JUST BEFORE THE first event in the 2009 World Series, Isaac did a makeover. He liked the grungy look he had before. Low maintenance, in particular, was appealing. But he thought a new look might help stir interest in sponsorship. Zoe helped. The shaggy shoulder-length hair he had grown during his sophomore year in college—a style which had made him the Lizard King—was now cut shorter, stylishly layered, and shaped, with a few feathery strands over his forehead. The haircut, Prada eyeglasses, and more stylish knit shirts, all together, so transformed him in appearance that several serious players in the tournament, whom Isaac knew quite well, now underestimated his play, because, to his surprise, they had no inkling who he was.

By the time of the final table, for the second time in the three years of his major tournament career, Isaac had the biggest of the nine remaining stacks. In second place was Vitaly Lunkin, a Russian champion in the game of *renju*, a game like *gomoku*, played with black and white pebbles on the same grid as the more ancient game of go. In *renju*, as in go, the contestants have complete information about the progress of play, and luck is not a factor. In poker, where incomplete information and luck are both important to the logic of betting, it seemed to follow that Lunkin would be tight, as he appeared to be, the kind of player people call a rock.

In his late thirties, he had thick features and a saturnine expression, which varied little over the course of the match. Most tellingly of all, he wore a fanny pack. His age, demeanor, and taste in games and accessories all seemed to promise that he would not bluff as much as poker requires. When the number of players dropped off at the end of the match, and when the blinds rose in proportion to the size of the stacks, if Lunkin did not bluff as much as everyone in the new generation of math nerds knew that he should, this would favor Isaac.

Early that day, angling for a more decisive advantage, Isaac played three huge pots. The first he lost. This doubled up Greg Raymer, a former patent attorney at Pfizer who had won the Main Event in 2004. Giving any opponent half his chips would have been bad enough, but this time Isaac had to lose while Raymer stared at him with holograms of lizard eyes, his trademark eyewear, over the lenses of his shades. Luckily, in his next two big pots, Isaac came back, nearly doubling his own stack twice.

Lunkin, meanwhile, used the tightness of his image, betting just enough to discourage a call and showing his cards only once in six hours. With utterly different styles of play, after seventy-seven hands and five eliminations, Isaac and Lunkin had returned to where they started, first and second place.

On the seventy-eighth hand, Isaac had pocket nines, and Lunkin, as a four-to-one dog with suited connectors, rivered the nuts. Isaac lost less than he might have, because he avoided a trap on the river, but Lunkin took the lead. Now, as chip leader, Lunkin came in for a raise three hands in a row. When Isaac decided to challenge this new aggression, Lunkin three-bet, all-in, over the top of Isaac's million-chip raise, and Isaac folded. Whether Lunkin had the cards or not, this betting was the opposite of his style of play so far.

Just when Isaac needed to secure his advantage for the end of the tournament, in short order he lost a substantial pot to each of his opponents and dropped back to the bottom of the stacks. Finally, he went all-in on a coin flip and hit lucky on the flop. He had been up, and down, and up again, and down. After ten full hours, he was up for the third time, and all three players stood within 1 percent of eight million chips.

A few hands later, Isaac eliminated Raymer when pocket nines held this time over pocket fives. But in the next hour, Lunkin, with his looser, more aggressive style, recovered from a two-to-one deficit and took the lead. Then Isaac shifted gears and came back for the fourth time, feeling more confident in his read of Lunkin's bluffs. After more than two hours heads-up, Isaac picked a spot to raise all-in, and Lunkin called his bluff with pocket tens, and won.

Eleven hours after the first hand at the final table, Isaac was trailing with only a third of the chips, when he found himself holding the king and the ten of spades, a good, strong hand in heads-up play. With the big blind now at 200,000 chips, Isaac made a standard bet of 400,000 on the button, and Lunkin made the standard call. The flop came K53, rainbow, leaving Isaac with the kings, top pair, with a better-than-average kicker, a four-to-one favorite against random opposition and a very favorable flop for Isaac. He made a slightly larger-than-average bet, 525,000, and then he called when Lunkin check/raised to 1.5 million. Isaac saw himself in a strong position, but he only called, hoping to get more chips in on the turn.

When the turn came 6, and threatened a possible straight, Isaac moved all-in over the top, after Lunkin opened with a bet of only half the pot. Lunkin seemed to have read Isaac as weak on the flop, and Lunkin's small bet looked like a weak hand, testing the waters. Isaac was hoping now that Lunkin would read his big raise as a bluff and call, as he had done before. The hope was that Lunkin had a strong enough hand to call what appeared to be a bluff. Isaac's chances of being ahead, against a random selection of hands, still were four to one. He was glad when Lunkin called. But Lunkin did not have a random selection of hands. He had pocket aces, which he now turned up. Isaac stood from his chair in disbelief and walked away from the table, dumbstruck to find himself a nine-to-one dog on the river.

Scott, Isaac's friend from college, was sitting with Zoe at the rail. When Isaac turned back toward the cards and looked down gloomily waiting for the river card to end the match, there was no point sitting down. He would have to stand up again in a few seconds, when it was over. The dealer was waiting to deal that last card, because the delay at this point makes good television. From the subdued murmur at Isaac's rail, Scott spoke up, jauntily asking, "Dare I say, 'One time'?"

Scott was joking. Players in Isaac's position often beg the dealer and the poker gods for the card they need. "One time!" they keep saying, hand after hand. They want the poker gods to come through with a long-shot winner, just this one time, but they ask this many times, and it gets more irritating every time you hear it. One of the players at the final table that day had offered a new theory about the expression. Maybe, for the truly devout, it really works. Maybe it only seems obnoxious and ineffective because the people heard saying it most often are the ones who have already used it up. If you still have your one time in reserve, if you have not used it in a particular tournament, it will work, just once. After their discussion of this theory, the players at the final table kept asking each other if anyone thought a particular situation would be a good spot to use the one time, and the unanimous conclusion of the group in all these cases was, no, you should save it.

So, when Scott piped up with his suggestion, Isaac had to laugh. He turned to Scott and Zoe, and said that this *would* be a good spot to use his one time. He gave a conclusive nod and said, with emphasis, "Ten! One time!"

Scott said, loudly again, with decisive calm, "I think we're going to use the one time here."

Zoe looked up, giggling, at Scott. She clapped and said, loudly, without a trace of irony, "One time!" You have to love Zoe for looking so hopeful, despite the odds. Scott, laughing, led the crowd in a shout, with his facetious inflection, "One time! One time!"

The crowd at Isaac's rail, with Justin and several of Isaac's friends, all shouted, "One time!"

But one of the Russians at the other rail objected. He held his right forefinger straight up, waved it at the dealer, and declared, "Noo! No one time."

Isaac was cracking up with laughter. Lunkin, who had stood, sat down again, looking nervous, clenching his right hand, knuckle to his lips. This card, if it was anything besides a king or ten, would win Lunkin $600,000. The tournament would be over. Both players seemed to agree that this was the point when superstitious body language becomes strictly necessary. Isaac was standing, because sitting would be an unlucky indication that he expected to win and keep playing, and Lunkin was sitting, because standing would indicate that he expected to win and end the match.

Isaac stood, arms folded, laughter starting to fade now into the smile of a nine-to-one dog being a good sport. He was grateful that the joke relieved the tension. It was a funny show.

But it was a slightly desperate joke, until the dealer laid the ten of clubs face-up on the felt. Ten, one time. Isaac shouted, "What?!" Both his arms shot straight up, instantly, over his head, as if Super Isaac might now soar around the room. Zoe did the opposite, her knees gave, and she doubled over with laughter, clapping and springing back to full height. Justin's face had broken into a huge grin. Isaac's friends could not believe he was back in the lead, again, after five swings down, that day, and five more up.

Lunkin looked stoic at the setback, smiling a hint of a bitter smile. He tugged his left earlobe.

Isaac said, "I guess that's my one time," and returned to his chair, still shaking his head.

Two hands later, Lunkin went all in, and now Isaac was the one ahead, one card away from winning the tournament, odds three to one in his favor. But Lunkin, this time, hit the lucky river, and shortly after that, he won a coin flip, again on the river, and took the first-place prize of $1.8 million. Both played well. The luck kept shifting.

Incontrovertible luck on the river, whether the luck is fading hearts or not, decides the fate of every player many times in every tournament. Isaac was exhausted after twelve hours' play and happy to have won the biggest cash in his career so far, $1.2 million. He congratulated Lunkin first and then he went to the rail to celebrate with his friends.

"The worst part," Scott mused, ruefully, "is wasting the one time."

Justin had to concur. "An unfortunate use of the one time."

As a former student of philosophy, Isaac agreed, and he put the paradox as a question for the ages, "How do I nail the one time and still not win the tournament?"

✳

THE FIRST SUMMER Isaac and Zoe were spending time together, he and two of his friends were renting the ground floor of a little house near campus in Providence. The window of the house next door stood about eight feet from Isaac's bedroom window, and his orange walls glowed even in the dark, but he was happy to be renting off-campus for the first time.

Zoe lived in Boston, and they visited each other as often as they could. After a few weeks sleeping on a crummy mattress on the floor, Isaac suggested that they might find something better. His income from poker made it silly not to buy what he really wanted. Though shopping for anything one minute more than necessary has always been a chore for Isaac, thoughtful attention to the bed he shared with Zoe made this excursion a forbidden celebration. They were in love. And they had fun, as the youngest customers in the store, checking out the high-end mattresses.

In Isaac's room, when they lay down together in their luxurious new bed, they joked about how settled they were getting in their nest, in his ugly orange summer digs, with dirty clothes strewn all around, and the best mattress they could find, silvery-blue satin sheets and all, plunked down, like its predecessor, without a frame, in the middle of the floor.

The act of laying claim in public to shared bedding, they both felt, was a virtual marriage. They were newlyweds. They liked it, to be joking this way. Next to their easy banter about wedlock, an engagement would have been beside the point. That night, after Isaac fell asleep, Zoe told me recently, she watched him breathe, his long, thick curls across the sheets darkly lustrous under the orange glow. She felt peaceful and newly alive.

※

THAT SPRING AND summer, in 2005, Isaac worked at the computer lab on campus, helping to design the bot for the Trading Agent

Competition, and Zoe, when she was staying at his apartment, sometimes played the poker bot from the University of Alberta. It was clear
to anyone interested that the poker problem would be solved by programmers, just as the option valuation problem had been solved by the
Black-Scholes algorithm in the 1970s, and the chess problem had been
solved by Deep Blue and others in the 1990s.

Chess bots were beating the finest players in the world, and poker
bots would be beating Isaac and his peers before much longer. The
days of financial success for poker pros on the internet, regardless of
the law, would end when the best bots could anticipate and outmaneu-
ver them. The financial incentive for this kind of programming is huge.

In the years since 2005 the bots have stopped losing to talented
beginners like Zoe. They have worked their way up to succeed at the
highest stakes in limit hold 'em. Now they are advancing through the
ranks of the no-limit game. It may not be very many years before an
honest game of hold 'em between unwired human players will be possible only in a secure room swept for electronic devices.

When Isaac started thinking seriously about the programming
of poker bots, in 2006, he was studying with one of the mathematicians who had made big money using the Black-Scholes algorithm on
options trading in the 1970s. Isaac was thinking that he might try to
design a program himself. But he soon discovered that the solution
would require years of concentrated work from teams of brilliant programmers. In the meantime, Isaac could be making better money using
his skills to play the game.

Clearly, the internet casinos will be coming down, just the way the
old brick-and-mortar casinos have kept coming down. The bots will
swarm over their human competition with no more mercy than the

bots in *The Matrix* or the chicken pox virus in Isaac's brain. When they do this, no doubt, Isaac will have to end his amazing run.

He no longer has much interest in a job testing video games for Nintendo. But he would love a position on the team that designs new decks for Magic. He still likes to play Magic online. In early 2013, he was the most highly rated player on the site he used.

❊

THE PLAY OF randomness in Magic and in poker differs categorically from the ironclad logic of chess.

Chance may be the opposite of causation. In physics and in evolutionary science, however, chance has become the matrix for causation. In a world of random subatomic events and random genetic combinations, logic itself, even in the purest mathematics, can no longer escape contradiction and incompleteness. This more contingent view of cause and effect and the more rigorous logic of probabilities have changed our ways of representing the world as much as any thinking since the Renaissance.

Poker players at the table work this problem.

❊

IN THE PANORAMA Towers on Dean Martin Boulevard, Isaac and Zoe lived high up with a vista of the city, the desert, and the mountains around them. The Strip lay at their feet like the set for a blockbuster movie, ersatz palaces, pyramids, monuments, and villas everywhere among skyscrapers, and inside them, thickets of real jungle flowers,

jewels, sharks, ungainly imitations of old sculptures, and flashy fountains with the most expensive lighting and accompaniment of overflowing schmaltz.

For me, aesthetic approval of the Strip feels like a sucker's trance
at the roulette wheel. Everything about the place is asking the visitor to
assume the position. But for Isaac and Zoe it is less an act of mayhem
on the unseasoned imagination than it is merely itself. When they lived
near the Strip and they were wondering what to do for their amusement, they had a running joke, that they should go get married at one
of the drive-through chapels.

What they really did, however, and I was happy to be with them
when they did, was eat. There was one place they could go at 3 AM
to have their choice of dozens of dishes no one between them and
Chinatown in New York City ever dreamed of getting. There was the
Vietnamese sandwich shop where they had lunch. There was a rundown mall just off the north end of the Strip, where you could get
Thai food as good as any and order wine from a list compiled by high-
end chefs who ate there. For almost any ethnic food you cared to eat,
there was a first-rate place. As for the high-end restaurants themselves,
Italian, French, or Japanese, chefs from other cities traveled there to
eat and learn. Isaac and Zoe ate as well as anyone I know.

But on Friday, April 15, 2011, Black Friday, poker on the internet
stopped cold. Most of the money in accounts online was frozen, out
of reach, or gone. For the second time, an action by the Department
of Justice froze a sum in the upper-six-figure range in Isaac's account,
though once again he was not alleged to have committed a crime. In
Mexico, Canada, South America, Australia, Europe, most of India,
and elsewhere, internet poker still ran, but not in the United States.

The case in court would take years. In late 2013, the players had not yet received their reimbursements. Effective regulation will take even longer. In any case, after the 2011 World Series of Poker, it was time for Isaac and many of his friends to move to where they could play online.

Later that summer, when their next move was a few weeks away, Isaac and Zoe were just out of bed, having coffee, still in their pajamas, and talking about their plans. The subject of residency in Malta came up, and Isaac mentioned that it might be easier for Zoe if they got married, that is, if she wanted to. He heard himself asking her this way, and he apologized. It just came out, he said. Zoe joked about it, the way they always had, and they agreed, in their pajamas on the couch, with their panoramic view of the city, the desert, and the mountains beyond, that it made sense now. It was time.

The wedding, though, logistics, date, location, guest list, everything on such short notice, looked impossible. They talked it through, suggesting this and that, and nothing seemed quite right. After a few days, one of them said, joking for the umpteenth time, they could just do a drive-through wedding at one of the chapels on the Strip. They laughed, as usual, but they agreed that this, in fact, was what they really wanted to do.

They loved their car, for one thing. It was a gold Prius they picked out the summer after Isaac's big cash in the Bahamas, in their second year together. The odd thing about it is that Isaac does not drive. He has never had a driver's license. He bought the Prius so that Zoe could drive it and he could ride along. She drove it then from Las Vegas, where they had bought it, back to Providence, where Isaac finished school, and, after graduation, back to Vegas again. The Prius was an emblem, an embodiment, of their bond, and this made it the perfect chamber for their wedding vows.

Zoe went online and narrowed the list of drive-through chapels down to three. They decided, after due diligence on the websites, to do the $40 Drive Thru Special at the world-famous Little White Wedding Chapel on South Las Vegas Boulevard. They made their reservation for September first at 3 PM. Nothing could be easier. They told Zoe's parents and us the good news, odd news, certainly, but good, and we were all delighted.

Now, Zoe needed a dress. Her first choice, in an elaborately beaded vintage style, she found at All Saints, an elegant shop in the new Cosmopolitan Hotel. She brought it home, and it was beautiful, but when she could not find a pair of shoes, it came to her that sitting in the Prius in these beads would not feel right.

Next, she went to the less exclusive Fashion Show Mall just off the Strip, and there she found a silk chiffon wrap, knee-length at the back, eight inches higher in front, the print mottled from brown to green to khaki, with a smattering of tiny gold sequins. This, with gold shoes, she decided, would be perfect for the Drive Thru Special in the Prius.

Still, something was missing, a pleat . . . not just a pleat, a pleat she sewed herself, with thread saved from her father's mother's kit, thread salvaged by her mother and passed along into the third generation. With this pleat sewn, the dress was ready. Zoe also wore a simple necklace which her father at twenty had given to her mother as birthday present.

Isaac wore black wingtips, like the ones I wore on a clear, summer afternoon under the chuppa held up by his uncles-to-be, when his mother-to-be wore a dress of ivory lace, in a garden overlooking the boats in Mamaroneck Harbor. Instead of a Brooks Brothers suit like mine, he chose indigo jeans with a chalky gray-blue shirt, opalescent when it shimmered in the desert sunlight.

For their nuptial lunch, at their favorite Greek place, they shared as a ritual of passage the flesh of single creature, a pink snapper baked in salt crust, sweet and tender, garnished with lemon and fresh, tiny sprigs of dill. The staff, whom they knew well, congratulated them and gave them glasses of Amalia brut, the only sparkling Greek wine made by the true *méthode champenoise.*

Then, they drove north on the Strip away from the elegant shops and restaurants, past the Wynn, past where the Stardust and the Frontier towers had come down with a sudden whoosh between midnight and dawn, beyond the rubble where the Rat Pack used to play in all the best hotels, now vanished like the Pack themselves, north, across Sahara, past storefront bail bondsmen, past burger chains, five miles, to a little white wedding chapel under a looming all-white sign with lettering now, oddly, gone.

The sign on the traffic island said, "Welcome to Fabulous Downtown Las Vegas Nevada." Technically, they had driven past the edge of Paradise, the unincorporated town where they lived, and they were back in the city of Las Vegas not far from where they had gotten their marriage license the day before.

They parked in the lot and stepped out of the air-conditioned car into the heat, hovering by then at 110 degrees. Zoe could not have been more beautiful than she was to Isaac in her wedding dress. Isaac looked sharp, too, with his shirttails flapping. But the wind was strong and hot enough to wipe the smile off anybody's face, and the neighborhood was worse when you were standing in it. There were tattoo

and body-piercing shops on both sides of the street. Next to the Silver
Spur was TOD Motor Motel, where vacancy appeared to be a permanent condition.

TOD, all caps, did not seem to indicate a person's name, but the
acronym Time of Death. Guests at TOD Motel, after their final repast
at Albo's Pizza, 99¢, could no doubt enjoy a final evening's entertainment next door, at Dino's Lounge, which is a dive bar with drunken
karaoke and with 1970s porn playing on a video monitor in one corner. Or they could go across the street to a gargantuan topless, bottomless cabaret, with hundreds of male and female dancers doing lap
dances around the clock for bachelors and bachelorettes.

Zoe and Isaac were too preoccupied to dwell on local color, though
they could not help but notice the scene basking in the glare around
them. The wedding chapel interested them more, and, at first glance,
it was a wreck. Though white, as advertised, the whitewash was now
badly weathered, and the roof gaped at the seams. The metal blinds on
the front windows, painted shut for years now, seemed to indicate a
history of misfortune.

It might not have seemed quite possible to anyone still sizzling on
the flattop of the parking lot, but inside was distinctly worse. Underfoot
the linoleum, which used to be off-white, had aged to yellow-brown
and cracked. It stank from disinfectant, which seemed somehow to
have made the surface grungier. The first whiff called to mind the
moment when one of a drunken wedding party loses his most recent
meal and slogs on to the altar.

Another couple in their wedding clothes sat on folding chairs in
a shabby office alcove to the right. Isaac and Zoe turned away and
wandered into the first chapel on their left, which resembled the inside

of a shoebox containing models of a podium with lectern and a prefab stained-glass window.

After they turned back into the fluorescent buzz of the common area, where an old computer blinked on a battered metal desk, they tried ducking into the second chapel, with a filthy green shag carpet, which was supposed to look like grass. The trellis with fake vines and flowers, placed as if to give the room a touch of life, suggested something more like rigor mortis. The third chapel, which was the most elaborate, had an aura of debunked illusion, like a movie set designed for filming in soft focus and dim light. With cheap pews, garish stained glass, and pulpit of composite board with wood-grain paper finish, this room was to an actual chapel as the Easy-Bake Oven is to the Viking Range.

Finally, they found a man who worked there. They asked him about their service, and he asked them, in a friendly way, what brought them to Las Vegas. When Isaac said he played cards for a living, the man said yes, as if he had been asked, he played as well. His wife nagged him—here, he gave a wink—to switch to the cash game, because he beat the play-money game for millions. The man knew, if he gambled, she would nag him worse. They had gotten married, he said, at the courthouse, and that worked for them. He shook his head, as if he might believe the opposite of what he was saying. But he was friendly, and his tone suggested the sincere belief that his good counsel would uplift the bride and groom.

When asked to check his list, he was surprised, as if this had not happened daily since he started working here, that Zoe and Isaac did not appear on the schedule. When they mentioned having reservations at the Little White Wedding Chapel, the man directed them without apology to another chapel, also little, also white, a few hundred yards away, on the far side of a HoJo's with a sign offering free margaritas to the newlyweds.

There was a bridal shop in that block, next to the Adult Superstore. Near the High Hat Motel, the Strip Centre advertised gold watches, slot machines, and a lounge, with a liquor store described on the sign as a miniature paradise. The Talk of the Town across the street advertised strippers, nude daily, for lap dances and—I would guess in this case that it is a beverage—deep throat.

The chapel itself was an improvement. The signs and the building, with its little steeple, were well painted and in good repair. Several kinds of real trees grew from the actual earth of the lot. Out front, in cast metal painted white, there were seven benches on a yard of AstroTurf, a fence with valentine hearts on top, quaint lampposts with three lamps on each, and dry fountains flanking the door.

At the billing desk inside, Isaac apologized for being late. The reverend, a calm, middle-aged lady with neat, straight, shoulder-length gray hair, said, Please, no problem. She would meet them at the window. She was welcoming and efficient.

They drove into the Tunnel of Love and saw, painted on the inside of the awning overhead, a dark blue sky with little gold and larger blue-white stars and cartoonish baby angels, golden-winged, some kissing, others dancing, some with harps. At the drive-through window, a female photographer in shorts and T-shirt stepped in front of the car. Reverend Belinda slid back her glass panel, leaned forth, smiled, and asked them, "Would you like for me to mention God?"

They said no, thanks. She nodded and spoke briefly, in a pleasant sing-song which made everything sound unremarkably benign, until the words about the rings and the instruction "You may kiss each other," with which they were happy to comply. The reverend promptly handed them an empty envelope and said her only compensation was the tip.

After they posed at the gazebo and beside the pink Cadillac with Elvis plates, Zoe took a photograph of their hands together with the rings. Then they headed south again, back to the Cosmopolitan, where, in their honeymoon suite, they shared a bottle of champagne on ice. The vintage they requested was 2005, their first year together. This, and the welcome privacy of their cool room, they enjoyed together from late afternoon until mid-evening, when they had a reservation for the tasting menu at Joël Robuchon, the only restaurant in Paradise ever to receive a three-star rating from *Guide Michelin*. After the bottle of champagne, they thought it best to take a cab.

In the main dining room, under a crystal chandelier suspended from the seventeen-foot ceiling coffered with gold trim, four crystal vases on the centerpiece held each a sphere of large pink roses, four dozen roses to the sphere. On each dining table in a little wide-mouthed vase was a circle of six more pink roses with a seventh, slightly higher, larger, and more fully opened rose at the center, the arrangement a perfect spherical cap.

The sommelier suggested starting with Sancerre, and Zoe and Isaac said just a glass, to sample with the bread. To drink with the rest of the meal, Isaac asked if there was something wonderful from the year 2005, and they were served a bottle of Chablis, which Zoe tells me was the most delicious wine that she has ever tasted.

The bread cart made the room's decor look meager by comparison: sheaves of wheat stalks in the center basket with *baguettes classiques,* surrounded by *batons*; loaves of fougasse, brioche, and sourdough, with poppy seeds, bacon and mustard, rosemary, Gruyère—two dozen kinds of bread, described by the server in English he made savory with terms of art in French.

Isaac and Zoe wanted everything, but they had to pace themselves, with fifteen courses yet to come. After Amalia brut at lunch, champagne in their room, now Sancerre, and soon Chablis, their resolve to enjoy as much as they could might have begun to wobble, but together they were strong.

La Cerise came next, cherry gazpacho, a dollop of sheep ricotta in the center, flecked with green crumbs of pistachio, a dish so smooth and sweet and tart, it seemed to say, I would have been the most delicious of thing on earth, if every course to come were not my equal.

Some of the highlights were caviar on panna cotta, seared scallop with coconut milk, sea urchin on fennel potato purée with anise orange, caramel parfait with hazelnuts and chocolate, and, to finish, for the truly indefatigable, among whom both the newlyweds could count themselves, the cart of macaroons, nougat, truffles, tartlets, and meringues. Marriage here in Paradise was good. Maybe they should reaffirm their vows, now that they saw precisely what the institution is about.

But it was time, instead, to catch their taxi back to the connubial refuge of their suite. Beyond the quiet threshold of the restaurant, Isaac, after more than his fair share of their champagne and still more of their bottle of Chablis, stepped out with Zoe onto the casino floor and heard, over the working of the slots, Sting on the speakers singing, "Don't stand so close to me." Isaac was ecstatic. His whole married life had been ecstatic. Now, he rhapsodized, out loud, about the genius of this song, the writing, the performance, the recording session, a topic about which, suddenly, he seemed to be summoning from the ether every known detail.

Zoe was happy when they slipped into the cab, because she knew from six years' experience that Isaac tended to be shy in cabs. He makes no conversation there. He answers a direct question with one quiet word or phrase. The passengers' assumption that it does not matter what the cabbie hears strikes Isaac as patrician nonsense. The personal dynamics of the space feel like a problem he has yet to solve. For the moment, this peculiarity of her new husband seemed to Zoe particularly appealing.

But, as he slid into the cab, the groom was warming to his topic so much that he lost his usual reserve and held forth loudly, steadily, on Sting's versatility in lyrical development and in his handling of genres, from punk and new wave, to rock steady, ska, reggae, and Algerian rai.

When they arrived at the Cosmopolitan, Isaac, still talking, paid the driver and walked, or was walked, into the lobby without missing a beat on the subject of Sting's recent foray into Elizabethan lute repertoire. In the elevator, just as Isaac was beginning to extol the daring of Sting's serious dedication to human rights, disaster relief, the environment, and world hunger, Zoe laid her hand on his shoulder while the door was closing, and said, gently, "OK, Isaac, that's enough on Sting."

He laughed, a little sheepishly, and they went back to being newlyweds.

※

SOON AFTER HE discovered doomsday on a cartoon show, Isaac at the age of four made up his doomsday poem, and in the dark of my soul, a part of me was glad. But I felt better when he let me know that he was ready for something else.

Toward the end of the dictation, he said, "There's a lot more that happens on doomsday, but most of it's not very interesting."

Poker on the other hand—thinking how to make luck happen—interests him for hours almost every day.

✳

SHUFFLE UP AND DEAL.

GLOSSARY

{**ALL-IN**} A player goes *all-in* by betting all the chips in his stack. Another player without as many chips is permitted to *call* the all-in bet, with his whole stack, and if that player wins, the original bettor loses only as many chips as the caller has put at stake.

{**BLIND**} The big *blind* and the small *blind* are obligatory bets placed by the two players at the left of the button before the cards are dealt. Blind bets differ from antes, because blinds are live bets that must be *called* or *raised* by players who want to stay in the hand. Blind bets are designed to guarantee a minimum level of betting. This guarantee is desirable for the house, which collects a percentage of every pot (see *rake*), and for the most skillful players.

{**BLUFF**} To present an imposing front, in the idiom of early nineteenth-century America. Because this kind of front is fundamental in poker, which was invented at that time, the game was sometimes called bluff. It was a much simpler game in its earliest form. Still, any competent player bluffs in a certain small percentage of hands. Not to bluff is a tactical error, because betting consistently in relation to the actual value of one's hand reveals the contents of the hands, so that opponents can easily avoid playing large pots when they are likely to lose. To bluff too often is also an error. The correct frequency for bluffing depends on the number of players and the character of their play.

{**BOAT**} A full house (see "List of Hands by Value," after the glossary).

{**BOT**} A poker *bot*, or robot, is an artificial intelligence program, the best of which can calculate probabilities in relation to hundreds of millions of data points per second, to determine the best action in betting. Poker bots are now beating the very best *limit* players and have begun to beat moderately skillful *no-limit* players.

{**BROADWAY**} The highest possible straight, from ten to ace.

{**BUBBLE**} The last unpaid place in a tournament. Sometimes, the player whose bubble is popped—the one they call the bubble boy—may be given a consolation prize, such as free entry into another tournament.

{**BUTTON**} A place marker which passes after each hand from player to player around the table to the left. In all but the first round of betting, the player on the button has the advantage of acting last, with maximum information about the other hands. He is the one who deals the cards in a home game, but not in a casino. A skillful player on the button may bet on the strength of advantageous position alone, despite a relatively weak hand.

{**CALL**} The choice to stay in the hand by contributing to the pot an amount equal to that contributed by the most recent bettor. For a player who has decided not to fold, a raise tends to be more useful than a call, because a raise puts pressure on the opposition, which yields information about the content of hands and the best strategy for betting. A player who calls very often puts himself at a distinct disadvantage and is known by the more skillful players as a calling station.

{**CARD SHARK**} A skillful player.

{**CARD SHARP**} A cheat.

{**CHECK**} To stay in the hand but not to open the betting.

{**CHECK/RAISE**} To *check/raise* is not to bet at first and to induce another player, who might not call an opening bet, to open with a bet, which the original checker then *raises*. A *check/raise* represents more strength than an opening bet, although this representation may be deceptive.

{**CONNECTORS**} Cards that follow in sequence, for example 7-8 or J-Q. Suited connectors belong to the same suit, thus increasing the chances for a flush as well as a straight.

{**CONTINUATION BET**} A player who makes a *continuation bet*, or c-bet, is continuing to apply the pressure from the bet he made in the previous round. The c-bet does not necessarily indicate improvement in the bettor's hand, but it increases the likelihood of a fold in response.

{**COOLER**} See *heater*.

{**DOG**} In a developing hand, a *dog* is an underdog, a player holding cards less likely to win.

{**DOUBLE UP**} Oddly enough, to win a hand and double the size of your stack.

{EQUITY} *Equity* extrapolates a player's likelihood of winning into a percentage of the amount at stake. There is almost never a chance of winning this percentage of the pot in a single hand, but over time, in a significant sample of results, theoretically, the sum of the player's equity in all hands played, if calculated correctly, would predict the player's total winnings for those hands.

{EXPECTATION} The amount of money a player calculates that he will earn in a particular hand or game. As with *equity*, though the actual results of the hands will vary, a correct estimation of this figure would be borne out, theoretically, by the results in a statistically significant sample of play.

{FADE} To *fade* a card, or several cards, is to avoid the card or cards that will give an opponent the winning hand. The verb, which seems to have been used first by craps throwers and then by pool shooters, appeals to the mentality of gamblers because it implies that the winner has a magical power, not just to profit from luck, but to generate luck, by fading disadvantageous cards out of existence.

{FLOP} The set of three common cards turned up on the board after the first round of betting in Texas hold 'em and similar games. The connotations of the verb suggest, most literally, the movement of the cards from face-down in the pack to face-up on the felt and, more figuratively, radical change (as when a politico flops from a progressive to a conservative position), loss of control (as when a fish flops on the deck), and failure (as when a play flops on opening night). The idea that anxiety about success can cause a flop sweat has caught on in theater but not in poker, though *sweat* is a poker term, which means to follow a player from the rail. Often, spectators who are sweating a particular player's game have bought a percentage of that player's potential winnings.

{FOLD} The choice to abandon the hand rather than contribute more to the pot.

{GAME THEORY} A branch of mathematics which formalizes the calculation of logic in gamelike scenarios, where success depends on decisions made by more than one person. Game theory has been applied in economics, business, philosophy, religion, political science, biology, and other disciplines. In poker, a common application of game theory is to form protocols for randomizing choices in ways that limit the value of strategic play by one's opponents.

{GANESH} (or Ganesha) A Hindu god with many names, the Remover of Obstacles, who presides over learning and fortune, in poker and in other business, and over the art of writing.

{GUTSHOT} A hand with a draw for one card which will complete a straight. Since the odds against filling an inside straight on the next draw are worse than ten to one, a rule of thumb for most poker players is not to bet on an inside straight. A double gutshot is a draw where either of two cards will complete a straight by filling one of two gaps in a longer sequence. The odds for filling a double gutshot are the same as those for filling an open-ended straight draw, where the two cards that will complete the straight come at either end of the sequence. Since the chances of hitting one of two cards you need are about one in six, for the turn and, if you miss the turn, about the same for the river, the pot odds after the flop for hitting one of the cards you need before the end of the hand are not quite one in three. Considering the further probability that your opposition may fold in response to your betting, the pot odds for a bet with a double gutshot, or open-ender, are sometimes better than even when the pot is large.

{HEADS-UP} Because it involves only two players, with a small likelihood of either player holding a very strong hand at any given time, *heads-up* play relies on strategic patterns in betting even more heavily than a game with more players. The patterns of betting are very different in heads-up play from those in games with more players.

{HEATER} A series of improbably strong hands and successful plays in a relatively short time. The term suggests that random events may appear to follow a pattern, as though governed, like thermodynamics, by discernible causes. A *cooler* is the opposite.

{HERMES} The ancient Greek god who presides over fortune and prosperity, in poker and elsewhere, and over the art of writing, among other things. His good standing among writers, poker players, and businesspeople also involves his powers as the god of misrepresentation and thievery.

{HIGH ROLLER} A tournament with a large buy-in. In a series of tournaments, when the main event has a buy-in of $5,000, the high roller may have a buy-in of $10,000. In other cases the buy-ins for high rollers may be as much as $100,000; $250,000; or even $1,000,000.

{HIGH STAKES} *High stakes* may be defined according to various standards. Most players online agree that a game with a big blind of $100 is a high-stakes game. In a game at those stakes, pots totaling more than $10,000 are commonplace. Everyone agrees that *microstakes* involve a big blind of less than a dollar, often less than a quarter, and sometimes pennies. A $1 big blind indicates a small-stakes game, although it is not unusual to win, or to lose, more than the average daily wage in this country during one session of no-limit hold 'em with a $1 big blind.

{HOLLYWOODING} In its older sense, in any sport, *hollywooding* is obnoxiously theatrical behavior during play, including talking smack, showboating, and so on. In a more recent sense, confined to poker, hollywooding is the slowing down of the last phase of the hand, by the player's acting as though he is reluctant to fold after his opponent has *raised* in response to his *bluff*. This kind of acting helps to hide how often a player bluffs, which is information useful to everyone betting against the player. The other players at the table find hollywooding, in this sense of the word, obnoxious, because it uses everybody else's time to purchase an advantage for one player.

{IMPLIED ODDS} A player's *implied odds* anticipate the size of the pot after future betting, should his hand improve. To decide a bet on the basis of implied odds, a player calculates both the likelihood of improvement and the likelihood of a fold in response to his bet when he improves.

{INDUCE} To *induce* (a *fold*, a *bet*, or, often, a *bluff*) is, by deception, to cause a player to make a mistake in one's own favor.

{KICKER} An unpaired card that supplements the value of a pair, or two pair. A paired king with a queen as a kicker, for example, beats a paired king with a jack as a kicker.

{LAW OF LARGE NUMBERS} This law holds that random events in a sufficiently large number of instances will tend to be distributed according to the relative likelihood of their occurrence. This law, fundamental to statistics, is the basis of the management of insurance companies and casinos, as well as for the calculations of individual poker players and scientists in many fields, including quantum mechanics, genetics, and medicine.

{LIMIT HOLD 'EM} A game which involves limited increments in betting. The limit game tends to be more closely tied to the quality of the actual cards than the *no-limit* game, because the limited amounts diminish the effect of bluffing. Because of this limited variation in betting, the poker *bots* could beat the limit game long before they could beat *no-limit*.

{LIMP} To call the big blind.

{MICROSTAKES} See *high stakes*.

{NO-LIMIT HOLD 'EM} A game which involves more highly developed and various strategies in betting than the limit game and generates much larger pots than those in a limit game with the same size blinds.

{NOSEBLEEDS} The highest of the high-stakes games, where the big blind may be $500 or $1,000.

{NUT LOW} The best possible low hand, in a game where the low hand wins.

{NUTS} The best possible cards to have in a hand, given the cards already turned up on the board. The term refers to a highly valued foodstuff collected and hidden by squirrels.

{OUTS} The cards that will move a particular hand from a losing into a winning position. The number of outs divided by the number of cards a player has not seen (i.e., forty-seven after the flop, forty-six after the turn) gives that player's probability of hitting an out on the next card revealed.

{PARADISE} Because *Paradise*, Nevada, which is the largest unincorporated town in the United States, contains the Strip, the core of what they call Sin City is in Paradise, not in Las Vegas.

{POCKET} A *pocket* pair is a pair with both the matched cards in the player's hand. The odds against being dealt a pocket pair are 16 to 1. The odds against being dealt a particular pocket pair, aces, for example, are 220 to 1.

{POT ODDS} Odds that represent the size of a player's bet in proportion to the total pot and compare this fraction to the probability of the player's winning. If a player has a one-in-ten chance of winning, his *equity* is 10 percent, and a bet that amounts to a tenth of the total pot makes the pot odds even. To place bets with less than even pot odds will be unprofitable in a statistically significant sample of play. When a bet is made for strategic reasons, such as a *bluff*, or a semi-bluff (in anticipation of *implied odds*), the likelihood of a *fold* in response to the bet is one of the numbers used in calculating the pot odds.

{RAINBOW} A selection of suits that make a flush unlikely.

{RAISE} The choice to increase the amount that every player must contribute to the pot in order to stay in the hand. A player uncertain of the relative strength of his hand may raise to test the quality of his opponents' cards.

{RAKE} The *rake* in poker is a certain percentage which the house collects from every pot as a fee for running the game. In games like craps, roulette, and blackjack, where there is no rake, the players, at a statistical disadvantage, bet against the house, and the mathematics and ethics that govern the betting of the house are like those of an insurance company. In poker, the house does not bet, but collects the rake, which makes the ethics and mathematics of running a poker room more like those of a landlord who rents property to a number of competing restaurateurs, the majority of whom will be paying rent while their businesses lose money.

{REPRESENT} To suggest by betting in a certain way the range of hands that justify such bets. A predictable pattern of representing hands is easily exploited by skillful opposition.

{RIVER} The fifth and last common card turned up on the board in Texas hold 'em. To *river* a card is to have that card turned up as the last common card.

{SATELLITE} A tournament in which the winner receives free entry into another tournament with a much higher fee.

{SHOWDOWN} A *showdown* comes after the end of the betting, when more than one player is still in the hand and the cards must show who wins. Most of the hands in a professional game are not shown. In this respect, betting in poker resembles the argumentation of lawsuits, most of which are settled out of court.

{SICK} In poker, a *sick* play is an unbelievably effective play. The term seems to have entered poker slang from the language of competitive skateboarders and surfers.

{TANK} In poker, to *tank* does not mean to be dishonest, as it does when a sports gambler complains that the better fighter has tanked the fight, or taken a dive, presumably into said tank. To tank, in poker, is to think. The tank in poker is where a player immerses his mind when he takes a long time to decide his next move. Some people are motionless and silent in the tank. Some fidget. Some handle their chips with great legerdemain. Some talk to themselves or to others. If the other player is already all-in, there is no need for a poker face in the tank. On the contrary, revealing behavior in the tank may generate a revealing response, a telling word or gesture. Tanking in hopes of getting such a response is a common ploy. The tank also may be required for a difficult mathematical calculation, for the construction of a story that explains the opponent's pattern of betting and behaving, or for the full anticipation of the various ways a hand might develop after a particular action. Going into the tank when one holds a winning hand may induce the opponent to call or raise. To go into the tank more than strictly necessary is bad manners.

{TELL} An action which inadvertently reveals something about the content of a bettor's hand: a gesture, a facial expression, a shift in the direction of the gaze, a change of posture, a tone of voice, and so forth. A false tell is a deliberate action designed to be mistaken for a tell. An ineffective false tell is a tell.

{TEXAS HOLD 'EM} The most popular form of poker in casinos, in tournaments, and online. It is described in chapter 1. The game seems to have been invented in Texas around 1900. It spread to Las Vegas casinos before 1970, gained popularity in the 1980s, and became an international craze in casino poker rooms, in tournaments, and online after the millennium.

{TOURNAMENT CHIPS} Markers of a player's success so far in a tournament, but they are not, like cash-game chips, redeemable for cash. The approximation of their value shifts over the course of the tournament, as explained in chapter 1.

{TURN} The card turned face-up after the flop, the fourth of the five common cards turned up on the board in Texas hold 'em.

{VALUE BET} A bet small enough to keep the odds favorable for an opponent to call. The concept is crucial in the logic of betting. A player who figures that he is certain to win, theoretically, places a value bet, which it is mathematically incorrect for the other player not to call. A *bluff*, when it is small, may look like a value bet and thus discourage a *call*. Conversely, a player with a very strong hand may place a bet much larger than a value bet to create the impression that he is bluffing.

LIST OF HANDS BY VALUE

THE NAMES OF the hands appear below in ascending order of value, which is the descending order of the probability of their occurrence.

HIGH CARD in an unpaired hand

PAIR

TWO PAIR

THREE OF A KIND

STRAIGHT: any five cards in a continuous sequence of rank, for example, four through eight, or nine through king

FLUSH: any five cards of one suit

FULL HOUSE: three of a kind and two of kind, also called a full boat, or a boat

FOUR OF A KIND, also called quads

STRAIGHT FLUSH: a straight with all five cards in the same suit

The standard **NOTATION** of hands is to use a number (2-9) or an uppercase letter (T-J-Q-K-A) to give the rank of the card, followed by a lowercase letter for the suit (c-d-h-s). The lowercase letters may be omitted where no flush is probable.